Making Gift Scrapbooks
in a Snap

20 perfect presents for family and friends

MEMORY
MAKERS
BOOKS

Executive Editor Kerry Arquette   **Founder** Michele Gerbrandt

Author and Artist Pam Klassen

Senior Editor MaryJo Regier

Art Director Andrea Zocchi

Designer Nick Nyffeler

Photographer Ken Trujillo

Contributing Photographers Brenda Martinez, Terry Ownby, Jennifer Reeves

Editorial Support Jodi Amidei, Emily Curry Hitchingham, Lydia Rueger, Dena Twinem, Janetta Wieneke

Making Gift Scrapbooks In A Snap

Copyright © 2004 Pam Klassen

Published by Memory Makers Books, an imprint of F & W Publications, Inc.
12365 Huron Street, Suite 500
Denver, CO 80234
Phone 1-800-254-9124

First edition. Printed in Singapore.

08 07 06 05 04 5 4 3 2 1

Library of Congress Cataloging-in-Publication Data

Klassen, Pam.
    Making gift scrapbooks in a snap : 20 perfect presents for friends and family / by
Pam Klassen.
        p. cm
    ISBN 1-892127-36-9
    1. Photograph albums. 2. Photographs--Conversation and restoration. 3. Scrapbooks. I.
Memory Makers Books. II. Title.

    TR465.K54 2004
    745.593--dc22

                                                        2004040153

Distributed to trade and art markets by

F & W Publications, Inc.
4700 East Galbraith Road, Cincinnati, OH 45236
Phone 1-800-289-0963

ISBN 1-892127-36-9

Memory Makers Books is the home of *Memory Makers*, the scrapbook magazine dedicated to educating and inspiring scrapbookers. To subscribe, or for more information, call 1-800-366-0405. Visit us on the Internet at www.memorymakersmagazine.com.

This book
belongs to :

_____

I dedicate this book to all readers who are inspired to create a scrapbook gift for someone they love.
Special thanks to the following artists whose talented work inspires great gift ideas: Peggy Adair, Becky Baack,
Debi Boring, Joy Candrian, Donna Dresp, Kristen Jensen, Franci Kettman, Julie Labuszewski, Susan McFall,
Shannon Taylor and Angela Siemens. Thanks to my editor, MaryJo Regier, who drove this book through production.
Thanks to my family for their love and support. With love, Pam

Table of Contents

Smart

BASEBALL

Friendship

High School

kind

Funny

Dedicated

richard

grandma

Loving

Communicate

Flowers

Selma, CA

Creative

Books

Caring

People
who
love
my

Introduction

Having been the Craft Editor for Memory Makers for six years, I have created many types of albums. I have also seen hundreds of little "specialty" albums—which have always attracted my attention and inspired me in the many albums I have made. In all my years as a scrapbook artist, I have learned that the gift scrapbook is the simplest album to make because it can be accomplished so quickly, an added bonus when you have a busy schedule and small children like I do. The gift scrapbook is also one of the most satisfying types of albums to complete because of the joy it brings to its recipient. Many scrapbookers shudder at the thought of creating a gift album in a single weekend. I can assure you that with a little preparation and planning, it can be done!

This book includes all the information you will need to organize your project before you begin. Design and journaling tips, as well as creation shortcuts, are sprinkled throughout to help you assemble your album quickly without adding excess bulk. Dozens of bonus album ideas for creating a truly personalized gift are also included. One of the most valuable tricks that I like to share for finishing a gift album in a weekend is to create simple yet effective continuity throughout the album. There are several tips included in this book to help you accomplish just that!

So gather your photos and supplies, clean off your workspace and use this book to inspire a one-of-a-kind gift that is certain to be treasured. Like me, you will soon realize the joy and appreciation a gift album can bring to loved ones and friends.

Pam

Pam Klassen
Author and Artist
Making Gift Scrapbooks in a Snap
20 Perfect Presents for Family and Friends

Getting started

There is no better reward for your scrapbooking efforts than when you see the happiness on someone's face when he or she receives a handmade gift album. The memories it creates are priceless. Gift scrapbook albums are highly personalized and center on a specific theme that is carried throughout the album by the use of consistent design elements, photos and journaling. Creating a gift album in one weekend may sound like a lot of work—if not impossible. However, you'll be able to get started quickly on a gift that lasts a lifetime with a few simple planning and organizational tips.

Start with a theme

Determining a gift album's theme requires some planning. First, ask yourself some questions. Who is the gift for? The album you make for a grandmother will look very different from an album made for a child. What is the occasion for the gift? Perhaps your gift album is to celebrate a new baby, a new marriage, a Christmas gift or just a personal way to say "thank you." Obviously, these types of albums would look quite different from one another. When do you need to have your gift completed? Whether you need to make a mini album in minutes or you have an entire month to organize your thoughts, ideas and supplies, your timeframe between scrapbooking and the gift-giving occasion will dictate how involved your design scheme can be. That is to say, if you have a tiny bit of time, make simple plans. More time allows for more elaborate plans. See below for theme album ideas which may spark inspiration for a unique gift album that is the perfect idea for a loved one or friend.

Theme album ideas

ABC	Club/organization	Inspiration	Shower
Advice	College	Love	Sisters
Amusement park/carnival	Daily life	Memorial	Snow
Animals or pets	Disney	Memories	Sports
Autumn	Dreams	Mother's Day	Spring
Baby	Easter	Moving	Storybook
Baking	Family	Nature/outdoors	Summer
Beach	Fantasy	Neighborhood	Teen
Birthday	Father's Day	Party	Thanks or appreciation
Calendar	Floral/gardening	Patriotic	Thanksgiving
Camping/fishing	Friendship	Picnic/BBQ	Traditions
Career	Graduation	Pool	Travel
Celebrations	Halloween	Religious	Tribute
Chanukah	Heritage	Retirement	Wedding
Characters	Hobby	School	Winter
Children	Holidays	Scouting	Zoo
Christmases Past	Home	Seasons	

Select photos

If you are compiling a history of a person—his or her life, career or marriage—you will need to gather photos from the recipient or family and friends. If you are creating a special gift, such as a friend's album, Father's Day gift or storybook album, you may need to determine and plan what pictures you need to take. Have your camera with you when the opportunity arises to get the needed pictures. Using random photos for a grandparents' brag book, flip calendar or treasured photo album may be easier to gather together, but may require searching through many photos to find the perfect photos to fit your theme.

If you are going to give a gift that showcases events throughout the year, such as a special trip, a season of sports, a year of school or a year-in-review, you will need to take pictures during the season or year.

When you create a gift for a single event—such as a shower, birthday or concert—you may want to plan your album beforehand to help determine the type of pictures you take during the event. Plan ahead for any photos that may need to be duplicated or resized. Use only the best photos and keep the number of photos to be used manageable to ensure the success of your weekend project. Finally, make notes about the memories each selected photo triggers to make journaling in the album quick and easy.

You may have a gift idea in mind for a holiday or birthday, but some of the best gifts are given for unexpected reasons. Just to show that someone is an important part of your life is a distinctive gift that never goes out of style.

Choose an album

There are many types of albums available. From a miniature size—at just 1" tall—to a large, 50-page spiral-bound album. Using a smaller album format helps make this gift easy to complete in a short amount of time because you are limited by the amount of space you have to fill. Your photos will often determine the size of the album you will need. A heritage project with many photos will often need a book with many pages. A book of school portraits may require a larger album, but to remember a fun barbecue or bridal shower you may need only a few pages.

Consider the style of album you might need. With three-ring binder, post-bound and strap-style albums, you can rearrange, remove or add pages as needed. The spiral-bound album doesn't allow you to move pages, but you can take pages out or make extra pages to add in. The stapled and accordion albums are perfect for single events and quick projects. If children will be looking at the album often, consider using PVC-free (polyvinyl chloride) page protectors to keep pages smudge-free. Whichever album you select, be sure it is made from archival materials that will withstand the test of time. Further, any materials used to create pages—from paper to stickers, die cuts and more—should be acid- and lignin-free. Use photo-safe adhesives and pigment pens for long-lasting results.

Knowing beforehand the number of photos that you wish to feature in an album will help you determine the number of pages needed in an album. You can purchase smaller sized albums on the Internet or at craft, scrapbook and specialty paper stores. Some select stationery and book stores also carry smaller, archival-quality albums. Consider an album with a blank cover if you want to decorate it to personalize your gift.

Gather tools & supplies

You probably already have some of the basic tools and supplies needed to put together your gift. Using acid- and lignin-free papers and photo-safe, archival-quality adhesives will ensure that your albums last. Scissors, a metal straightedge ruler, journaling pens, craft knife, paper trimmer and cutting mat are the only other basic tools or supplies you will need. Based on your design scheme, you may find templates, punches, decorative scissors, stamps or eyelet-setting tools useful. A number of projects in this book will feature some special tools that you may not have, but similar tools that you do own can be substituted without losing impact in the album.

The photos you select will help determine the color of paper and page additions that will complement your photos nicely. Choose two to four paper colors based on the colors most prominent in your photos. As a general rule, use light-colored papers for photos with dark backgrounds and dark-colored papers for photos with light backgrounds.

There are many scrapbook page accents available to give your gift a unique look, including colorants, embellishments, stickers and die cuts. Obviously, the page accents used in a Father's Day gift album will and should look much different from page accents for an album celebrating a baby's first year. Let the theme of your album and your selected photos and paper colors direct your choice of page accents.

Consistency and simplicity are the most important considerations when selecting coordinating page accents. First, be consistent in your album design by showing the same or similarly styled page accents repetitively throughout the album for a unified look. And second, keep page design simple. If you start introducing time-consuming scrapbook techniques into your gift album, your weekend project could easily become a multiweek or monthlong undertaking.

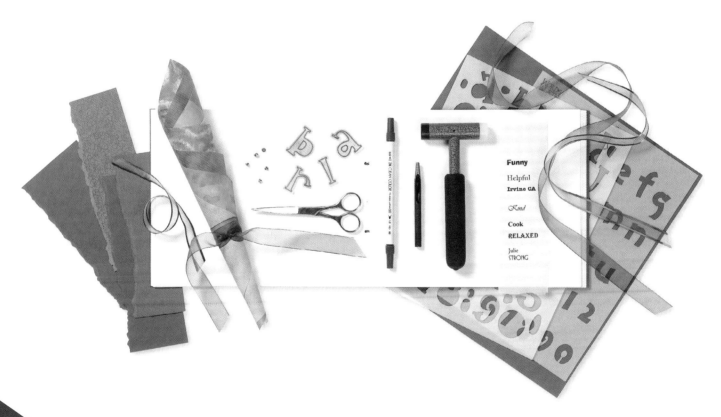

Put it all together

The key to completing a gift scrapbook in a weekend is organization. Once you have determined the album's theme, selected photos, chosen an album and gathered tools and supplies, let the creativity begin!

First, consider a title page. Will you decorate the album's cover as a title page or will the album's first page be the title page? Whatever you decide, the title page or album cover is a good place to introduce the color and design elements that will run through the entire album.

Next, determine the album's layout or arrangement. Will photos be presented in chronological, sequential or random order? Will you feature one photo and one quote per album page spread or will you weave a story throughout the entire album? Working in spreads, loosely place photos and mock journaling blocks on the album pages in the order you'd like them to appear. If possible, sketch your layout.

Finally, use your layout to help create a repetitive page design or to guide the placement of your page accents while focusing on the theme of the album. Pair the photos with papers and page accents for each album page, opting for placements that look balanced and draw focus to the photos. When you're happy with your album's layout and page design scheme, assemble your album working in spreads to keep a consistent flow going. Don't fill the album too full; pages should lie flat when it is opened.

The designs in this book can serve as a guide or starting point for inspiration. You can adapt most themes, designs and ideas to fit your own personal style as well as that of the loved ones and friends in your life.

The gift of giving

Your weekend labor of love will provide its just reward: giving the gift to an unsuspecting loved one or friend. Put some thought into a creative presentation of the album. Take time to wrap your gift in a special way.

Before you wrap the gift album, personalize the gift by creating a dedication page in the front of the album or include a separate page about yourself, the author of the album, in the back of the book. Include the reasons you've created the gift.

Create a box to hold the album or use nice tissue paper and tie a bow with a satin ribbon. If you are going to mail it, wrap the album in bubble wrap and mail it in a snug box to avoid content shifting. Your gift will be cherished for years to come.

ORGANIZATIONAL CHECKLIST

Photocopy this convenient checklist—for each gift album you are creating—to help you stay organized and to gather the materials you'll need to successfully complete a gift scrapbook in a weekend.

Start with a theme
❑ Decide on the theme of the album (see page 8)

Select photos
❑ Gather all photos to be included, make any copies and size adjustments needed (see page 9)
❑ List all the journaling to be included (see page 9)

Choose an album
❑ Select the type and style of album best suited to your project (see page 9)

Gather tools & supplies
❑ Gather all tools and supplies (see page 10)
❑ Make sure all tools are clean and in good working condition
❑ Shop for any needed papers or supplies (see page 10)

Put it all together
❑ Make sure you have a clean, organized workspace
❑ Arrange all supplies for easy availability
❑ Consider making a title page (see page 11)
❑ Determine the album's layout or arrangement (see page 11)
❑ Loosely assemble the album's contents and insert onto pages (see page 11)
❑ Sketch the layout for your album to determine where all pictures and journaling will go (see page 11)
❑ Assemble and finish your gift scrapbook in a weekend (see page 11)

The gift of giving
❑ Put some thought into a creative presentation of the gift (see page 12)
❑ Include a dedication or author's biography (see page 12)
❑ Wrap the gift (see page 12)
❑ Pack for shipping, if necessary (see page 12)
❑ Give the gift and enjoy the happiness! (see page 12)

CHAPTER 1

Fill-in albums

The fill-in album, like most gift albums, is designed with a consistent theme that runs throughout the book. What makes this album unique are the blank spaces for photos and journaling which you provide for the recipient through your page design. The recipient of the gift then "fills in" the pre-designed album with photos and journaling. This is one of the easiest albums to create because there are no photographs to organize.

When designing this type of album, be sure to leave enough room on the pages for the recipient to add his or her photos and journaling. Depending on the type of fill-in album you decide to make, some forethought into the album's design will be necessary. For example, a year-in-review album would need at least 12-24 pages to help represent the 12 months of a year. A bridal shower album may need spreads for a guest list and photos, game playing, gift opening, refreshments, favorite family recipes, etc.

Whatever the theme of your fill-in gift album, think about the type of event or occasion to be documented and plan accordingly.

Year-in-review
HIGHLIGHTS OF FAMILY LIFE

A year-in-review fill-in album is the perfect way to record memories and remember details of a year of family life. Simple, everyday details are often overlooked. By creating an album that provides a place to record everyday facts and photos, you create a wonderful time capsule. To save time, we used a pre-made, stitched paper. By cutting down a sheet of pre-stitched, 12 x 12" paper to fit a small album, you'd have extra paper left over to create journaling windows. Keep the stitched look throughout the album, changing the paper color to reflect the month of the year. Include a bag of decorative clips with the gift so journaling can be added easily.

Photos: Chelle Sugimoto

The *year-in-review album* does simply what it says: reviews the year. This album can be assembled to review by week, month or season. A good time to give this gift is at the beginning of a new year. Create this album during the summer so it is ready during the busy holiday season. The album you choose for this project needs to have enough pages in it to cover an entire year. Include a note with your gift with instructions for how to fill the pages with photos taken during that month or season.

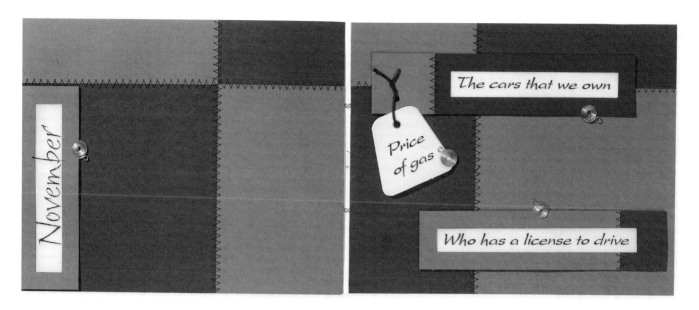

Although the color changes throughout the album, covering each page with the same paper style gives the album a consistent look. Put all of your journaling on vellum behind windows that are cut from stitched-paper remnants. Cut windows out of paper strips with a craft knife. Size your computer journaling to fit inside the windows, keeping the font consistent throughout the album. Adhere journaling blocks to the pages with self-adhesive foam spacers. Attach journaling tags with paper wire.

WHAT YOU'LL NEED

Album (Kolo)

Stitched paper (DMD)

Vellum paper for journaling

Letter stickers (Wordsworth)

Tags (DMD)

Paper wire (DMD)

Self-adhesive foam spacers
(All Night Media)

Spiral clips (7 Gypsies)

Scissors

Graphing ruler (C-Thru Ruler)

Craft knife

1 Put adhesive around entire edge of the album page. Position stitched paper on top of page, aligning stitching in the desired position on the page. Trim off 9¾" in length to fit album.

Organization tip

Separate all stickers, die cuts, patterned paper and page accents by theme to make it easy to find the perfect item for each album project.

Shortcuts

Use precut papers from a pack that contains a variety of colors. This saves time cropping to fit.

Sticky-faced stickers are an easy way to add decorative elements to the page by enhancing with beads, glitter, chalk, tiny glass marbles, shaved ice or metal flake.

2 Using scissors, trim stitched paper to fit scrapbook page.

3 Create journaling block on vellum. Make a window from stitched-paper remnants by using a ruler and craft knife to cut out an opening to accommodate the journaling.

Design tip

Choose a computer font that coordinates well with the style of page accents or theme used in your album.

4 Surround the reverse side of the window with adhesive, then adhere vellum journaling to back of window. Add self-adhesive foam spacers to back of window before mounting onto page for depth.

Seasons in review

Adding glitter to sticky-faced stickers is a quick-and-easy way to decorate this seasonal album. The pages are covered with patterned vellum, then torn mulberry strips are adhered to pages. Add an appropriate verse, quote or poem for each season. You can leave several pages open for pictures and journaling.

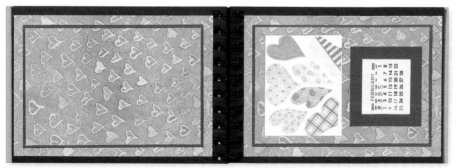

Personalize a family album

By using precut papers from a pack that contains a variety of colors, it's simple to finish twelve months. Mat paper with coordinating cardstock. Cut a window, line with white paper and decorate with vellum stickers appropriate for each month.

Calendar inspired by Judy Martin; Photo: Richard Gerbrandt

Other album ideas

BABY'S MILESTONES

Create pages that include a place to record a baby's monthly development.

HOME AND NEIGHBORHOOD

Design an album to document your home or neighborhood events during the different seasons.

GUEST REGISTER

A fun way to remember visitors. Leave this album out for guests to journal about their visit.

EVENT CALENDAR

Create an album for the person who likes to journal. Provide daily journaling boxes to fill in.

Single event

PERSONALIZE PAGES FOR A BRIDAL SHOWER

This project is fun and easy when shared by the guests at a bridal shower. The bonus is the personalized pages the bride will receive as a gift. Pictures taken at the event can easily be added later. Be prepared at the shower with basic scrapbook supplies, such as scissors, adhesive and journaling pens. This project becomes even easier when you choose a kit that contains the album and all coordinating decorations. For guests who are not creative, kits contain idea books.

Photo: Elizabeth Friesen

WHAT YOU'LL NEED

Scrapbook kit (Hot Off The Press)

containing an album (DMD)

⅛" hole punch (Fiskars)

¼" hole punch

Photo splits

The *single-event album* captures the memories of a special event and helps them last a lifetime. If the album is made prior to the event, try to anticipate what pictures might be taken to help decide on the amount of pages needed and the style of album to use. Think small for these albums, as most don't contain a lot of pictures.

Request by invitation that each guest bring a recipe or advice for the bride. Add these to the pages they create. Make sure there is a workstation for everyone. Cut out paper accents beforehand to make assembly of the pages speedy. If you use a spiral-bound album, have guests work with their layouts on paper that is the approximate size of the page. After completing the layouts, give everyone time to adhere them into the album.

1 Tear a horizontal strip out of the middle of the decorative paper.

Shortcuts

Remove pages of your album to use as plain cardstock when you have extra pages.

Use the same simple border design throughout the entire album to give your album consistency and save time.

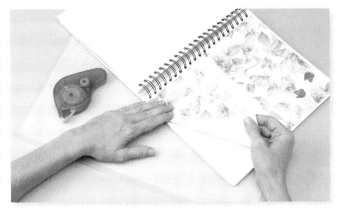

2 Back torn edges with adhesive tabs and punch with a ⅛" hand-held hole punch approximately every 1" along both torn edges, alternating alignment from top to bottom.

3 Adhere upper and lower edges of both larger pieces of torn paper to the album page, leaving ⅛" of top and bottom of album page showing.

Other album ideas

GRADUATION

Create a page for a copy of the diploma and leave room for well-wishes or life or career advice.

BIRTHDAY, ANNIVERSARY OR RETIREMENT

Make this album ahead of the event and the guests at the party can sign their wishes or record their most fond memories.

SPORTS EVENT

Create pages for memorabilia, the tickets and program.

GARDEN PARTY

Use products that reflect the theme of the album.

4 Stitch fiber through top and bottom holes using a small piece of wire as a needle folded in half near the end of the fiber. Wrap the fiber ends around brad fasteners at each end of the stitching.

Journaling tips

A variety of phrases and words on stickers is available for quick journaling solutions. Attach a letter of congratulations inside a celebration album for the recipient to read at a future time.

A wedding gift to treasure

The richness of gold against black pages makes this album a classic. After embellishing the strips of decorative paper with stickers, add photo corners for a quick way for the couple to add photos.

Photo: Intogrity Photography

Design tip

Keep page accents simple. A classic look will hold up better over the years as trends continue to change.

Send a gift home with each party guest

Here is a quick and simple idea that can be reproduced several times. Punch a hole in the same location in each page except the front and back. When you stamp on the front and back page within the punched opening you can see the design on all the pages. Design the cover to fit the party's theme.

Photo: Karen Gerbrandt

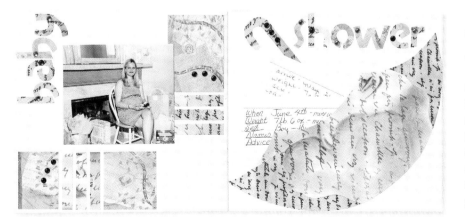

Create a memory for the new mom

Collage-style papers add interest to this album. Cut out template letters and create a pocket for advice. Make extra pocket pages to hold congratulatory cards for the mom-to-be. Embellish with rhinestones, using an adhesive that will hold them permanently.

Photo: Susan Gerbrandt

Timeline

FILL IN MEMORIES FROM A BABY'S 1ST YEAR

A fill-in baby album makes a perfect gift for any expectant mother. You don't even need to know if the baby will be a boy or a girl to complete this type of album long before the baby is born. Try using a color palette that is generic or unisex for paper selection. Paper shades should be similar throughout the album. Mixing bright papers with pastel papers will ruin the album's "pulled together" appearance. Three-dimensional stickers are the perfect embellishment for adding variety to patterned vellums. Using stickers from just one manufacturer will help give the album continuity in design.

Photos: Pamela Frye Hauer

The *timeline album* includes pictures and information that may span over a person's life or a specific period of a life—in this case, a baby's first twelve months. When creating a fill-in timeline album, use your imagination to put yourself in the gift recipient's shoes. Try to determine or anticipate what photographs the gift album recipient may have or be able to take to help you make choices about the content of the album.

WHAT YOU'LL NEED

Album (Mrs. Grossman's)
Patterned vellum papers (EK Success)
Silver paper (Bazzill)
Complementary-colored cardstock
Dimensional stickers (Meri Mori)
Decorative scissors (Family Treasures)
⅜" wide ribbon (Robin's Nest)
¼" round hand punch
Vellum adhesive (3M)

For consistency, use just one style of decorative scissors (in this case, scallop scissors are used) to cut photo mats and title and journaling blocks. Use the scalloped trim throughout the album to help tie all the pages together. Strategically place accented page titles, page accents, journaling blocks and photo mats in chronological or otherwise-logical order throughout the album.

For a unified look, preprint journaling blocks with a computer for the new mother to fill in. Use just one computer font; mixing and matching different computer fonts takes away from a unified look. Try to match the style of the computer font to the style of the patterned papers or page accents for simple style success.

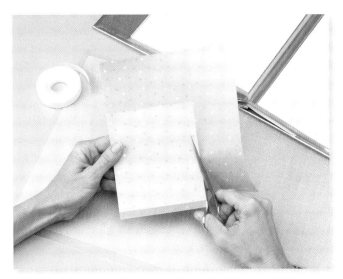

1 Cut a 4 x 6" white mat from cardstock. Apply small strips of vellum adhesive to the white mat. Adhere vellum and cut around mat.

Shortcuts

Select the colors for your album by the sticker accents used in the design.

Choose only one style of decorative scissors to use as an accent design throughout the entire album.

Other album ideas

ANNIVERSARY

Create pages to highlight a couple's life together.

TRADITIONS

Create an album that the recipient can fill in with photos and journaling about family traditions.

MY CHILDHOOD HOME

Allow spaces for photos and journaling.

FAVORITE FAMILY STORIES

On one side of a spread, leave a place for the family member's photo and a place for his or her story on the other.

AUTOGRAPHS

A place to keep cherished signatures of musicians, athletes, celebrities and authors; can include any event photos and memorabilia, such as ticket stubs, programs, etc.

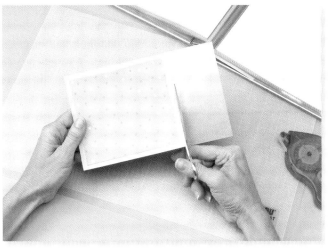

2 Mount mat on silver cardstock, leaving a ¼" border around the edges.

3 Trim around the mat with decorative scissors, lining up each cut with the previous design made by the scissor stroke.

Organization tips

Keep all of your materials together in one place to make it easier to work on your album whenever you have a few spare minutes.

Create a question & answer book

Purchase or create an album with journaling pages between each scrapbook page. This makes the perfect place for each grandparent to answer questions you've written in this book. Brainstorm about questions you'd love to ask by anticipating answers that future generations may find very interesting. For a truly endearing touch, mount matted photos of you with your grandparents or your children with their grandparents on the scrapbook pages. Keep the page design simple and repeat it in different colors on each page for variation.

Help a child learn her family tree

Here's a simple family tree that won't overwhelm young children with too much information. Begin by cutting a simple branch from paper for each page. Attach ribbons that hold a cardstock nameplate for each relative. Decorate the tree branches of first-generation photos with a single punched leaf. Likewise, decorate the tree branches of second-generation photos with two punched leaves and so on. You can add the names of the relatives you know, leaving room for the photos that you may not have on hand to add at a later time.

Journaling tips

For fill-in albums, it is easy to get ideas for your journaling from existing Life Story or Baby Album books. Select journaling ideas or alter them to personalize your gift.

Miscellaneous

FILL IN MEMORIES FROM YOUR TRAVELS

There are plenty of pages to fill with pictures and memorabilia in this unique three-paged, fold-out album. Use quick and easy stickers to identify each state along with appropriate state symbols and trivia. Find additional facts and information about each state that you visit to add to the album, either online or from travel brochures.

Get the inspiration for a variety of additional albums by gathering information from family and friends. When you plan for a gift, think of the pictures and events that are special to the recipient and create an album he or she can fill easily.

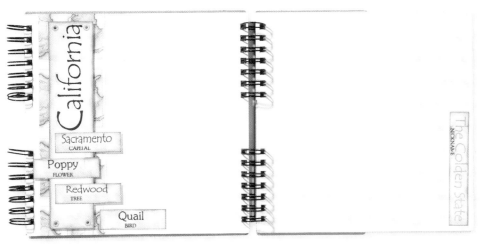

Highlight each state's information by mounting sticker titles on mats that have been inked with a stamp pad. Add hand-made eyelets to the corners of the mat. Mount the titles on theme paper using self-adhesive foam spacers. Coordinate the colors of ink with the sticker colors. For facts that are not in sticker form, print on vellum in a font similar to the look of the stickers.

WHAT YOU'LL NEED

Album (7 Gypsies)
Decorative paper (PSX Design)
Stickers (Destination Stickers and Stamps)
Colorbox ink pads (Clearsnap)
Vellum for journaling
¼" hole punch (Fiskars)
⅛" hole punch (Fiskars)
Metallic marker (Sakura)
Scissors

Design tip

Finish the edges of your pages or a mat with hand-drawn lines. As the lines cross each other, it adds a simple design.

Organization tip

The tools and supplies you use most often should be stored close to your workspace for easy access and quick scrapbooking.

1 Cut large mat 2 x 8½" and small mats to fit sticker size. Rub the edges of each mat with an ink pad.

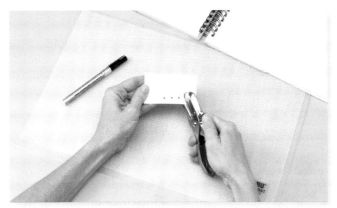

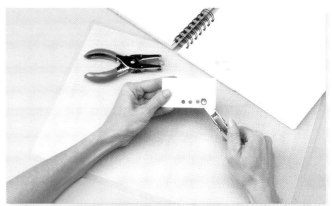

2 On a length of paper, color a ⅛" wide strip with metallic marker. Before punching, back the strip with adhesive tape. Using a hand punch, punch ⅛" holes centered in the inked color strip about ¼" apart.

3 Center the opening of a ¼" hole punch and re-punch over the ⅛" hole to create a faux eyelet.

Other album ideas

ABC ALBUM

Add letter-related items to each page, leaving room on the pages for pictures to be added.

SCHOOL PORTRAITS

Use school-theme page accents to decorate pages for each school-year portrait.

PET ALBUM

Create an album for someone's precious pet.

A DAY IN THE LIFE OF A CHILD

Make this album with photos in it, leaving the story to be filled in by the recipient.

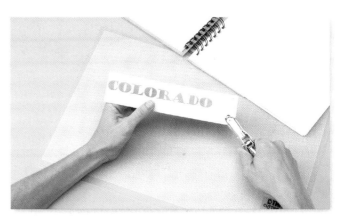

4 Remove adhesive backing and adhere these to the corners of your title mat. Re-punch through center of the eyelets with the ⅛" hole punch, punching through cardstock to finish the "eyelet."

Shortcuts

Keep your album simple and focused by using theme page accents. Gather all your scraps of patterned paper in one color to decorate an album. The repetitive use of color will create consistency and no shopping will be necessary.

Record the achievements of goals and wishes

A fun way to visually keep track of the achievement of someone's goals and wishes. Begin with the information to complete this album. Rub an ink pad lightly over your page, creating a simple background. Stamp your title and journaling block. Add sticker eyelets; punching out the center of the eyelets gives them depth. Encourage the recipient to record goals yearly.

Personalize an autograph book

This little album is ready to fill with autographs at a favorite amusement park, made quick-and-easy with a book of coordinating products. Cut background paper to fit page, mount on darker background and add mat for journaling and photo. Embellish with coordinating cutouts. A perfect album for sporting events, too.

Photo: Kris Perkins

Collect advice from family members

This type of fill-in album can contain photos and have pages ready for journaling. A great gift for the graduate, mother-to-be or a bride and groom. Tear journaling blocks to put on top of bright backgrounds. Punch holes near corners and insert paper strips, covering corners. Stamp names and add photos of family members.

Planned photo theme albums

The focus of this album is a specific event or topic and requires gathering and organizing of photos for that event or topic. In essence, you'll have a pretty good idea what photos you will use in a planned photo theme album. Creating a consistent design throughout this album helps the images stand out and makes it easy to complete. Personalize your gift by gathering additional information from the recipient.

When designing a planned photo theme album, you will begin by selecting a theme that will help showcase specific photos from those you have on hand. Themes can include anything from buying a new pet to remembering a trip to watching a birthday girl grow up or creating a tribute to someone you love. If you're stumped on topics, review the list of theme album ideas on page 8 and you'll be sure to find the perfect theme to fit the photos you have for a unique gift.

Start planning now so you'll have plenty of time to gather materials for an upcoming gift-giving occasion!

Single event

RECALL THE FUN OF A NEW PUPPY

Make photos of a beloved pet the focus of your album by creating a simple and subtle background. Wrap fibers around two sides of each page as a quick way to embellish this album.

Photos: Debbie Mock

The focus of the *single event album* is to capture the memories of a special event or occasion. Gather the photos and collect any information that will personalize your gift. Repeating a design throughout helps you complete this album quickly.

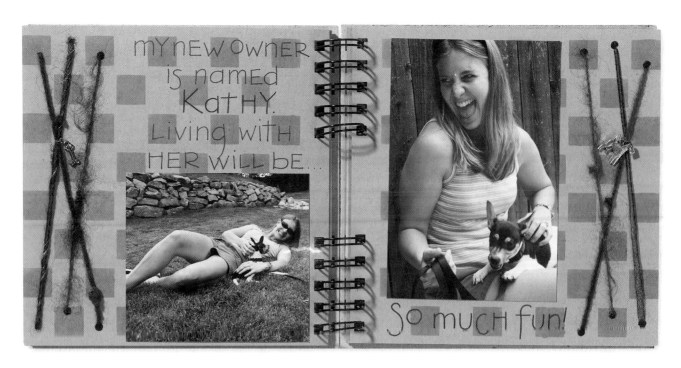

WHAT YOU'LL NEED

Album (7 Gypsies)

Stencil (PrintWorks)

Brown ink pad (Close To My Heart)

Makeup sponge

¼" hole punch (Fiskars)

Fibers (Fiber Scraps)

Jump rings (Westrim)

Charms (Boutique Trims)

Removable artist's tape

Needle-nose pliers

Scissors

Decorate a quick background by rubbing an ink pad over the full-page stencil. Use removable tape to hold your stencil in place while inking. This background accent method makes completing several pages a snap. It's simple to embellish two sides of your page at once. Simply punch random holes at both ends of a page and string fibers through, adding charms on both sides.

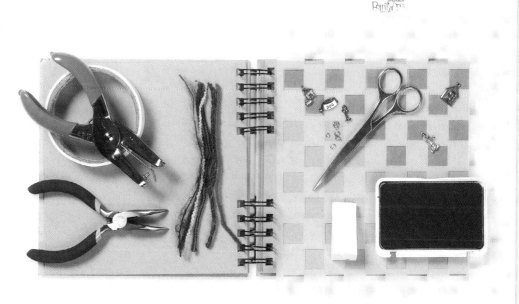

Organization tip

Clean up tools and supplies after using them. It will keep your work area uncluttered and make it easier to find what you need. Taking time now will save time later.

1 Line up the template square with the page and adhere to the page from the back using removable artist's tape. Rub ink pad over the entire page, making sure all openings are inked.

2 Punch three to four random ¼" holes at each end of the page.

3 String fibers through punched holes. Clip fibers close to the knot after tying the ends together.

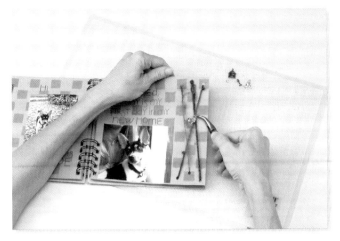

4 Using needle-nose pliers, twist open jump rings to attach charms where fibers cross. Attach charms on both sides of each page.

Other album ideas

TRIP TO THE ZOO

Help a child relive memories of a fun event and teach animal names and facts.

FIRST DAY OF SCHOOL

Put the events of the first school day of each year into an album chronologically. Use this album to review each school day with your child.

FISHING TRIP

Create an album that shows just how big the catch was.

HIKE IN THE MOUNTAINS

Relive a special trip. Include pressed flowers and leaves into your album to remember the day.

Shortcuts

Create handmade background pages by simply pressing your ink pad onto the page. Make an all over background or just a border. Mount photos directly to scrapbook page without matting to save time.

Photo tip

Reduce photos by making color copies, or use a computer, scanner and printer to reduce and print. When using a photo-duplication machine, you must have a photographer's release to copy professional pictures.

Gift for the new couple

This miniature version of the wedding album, created by Angela for her daughter, is quick, easy and elegant. Tear random edges of mulberry paper and adhere to page. Add photos that have been reduced in size. Embellish with skeletonized leaves and add letter stickers using self-adhesive foam spacers for dimension.

Photos: Angela Siemens, Manuel F. Sousa
Album: Angela Siemens

Remember the highlights of a trip

Joy created a beautiful memory of a trip her husband took. Tear paper for photo mat and design elements. Use a sewing machine to attach paper to pages. Print trip details onto vellum and mount each with a brad fastener.

Album: Joy Candrian

Timeline

FAMILY PROVIDES MEMORIES FOR AN ANNIVERSARY GIFT

Ask siblings and family friends to help with this album by writing down memories of the couple's marriage through the years. Separate all memories into similar ideas and match with related photos of each individual, the couple or the people who provide specific memories. Work chronologically, ending with the year of the anniversary. Include congratulatory letters from family and friends.

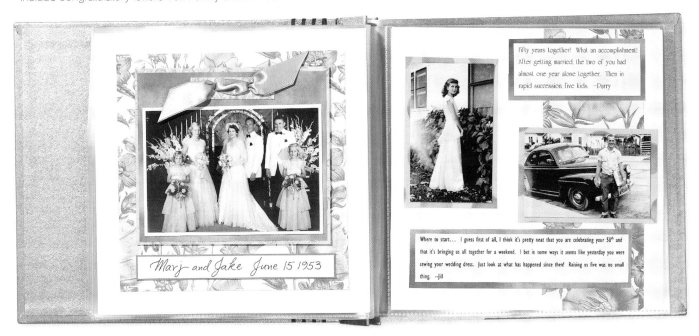

Create a title page using papers that will continue throughout the entire album. This page sets the design style for the entire album. Mat the photo twice, adding a decorative ribbon tied in a french knot. Select three to four colors and patterns to use throughout the entire album, using masculine colors on the pages for the husband and feminine colors on the pages for the wife.

I feel so lucky and blessed to have the parents I have! Your love and patience for me while I grew up made me who I am today. --Wendy

I will always remember how Mom & Dad's hospitality was and still is always there and ready to feed an extra person or the whole extended family and friends. I have always been amazed at your love of children, young and old, related or not. --Tony

So what would Mom and Dad say about that special day, their 50th wedding anniversary? It doesn't take much to imagine them saying: "Well, you just get up in the morning and put your pants on the same as every other day." Or, "Umm, I don't know, you just do it." These two aren't the celebrating, get wild and crazy types (which is okay with us). A night on the town is a Chinese buffet or a baseball game, especially if the Grizzlies are in town. Seems like we heard once that their first date together was a ball game. And what about the perfect meal? This has to be it--barbecued steaks, a green salad with lots of avocados, French bread and toothpicks for all afterward! And almost forgot, homemade vanilla ice cream for dessert. Bon a petit! --Parry

A *timeline album* is a chronological record of someone's marriage, life or career depicted through photos and journaling. These albums are the perfect place to include memorabilia, letters, cards or locks of hair. This album may require interviewing friends or family members to help document photos and gather journaling information.

WHAT YOU'LL NEED

Album (Mrs. Grossman's)
Patterned paper (Anna Griffin, Colors
By Design, Frances Meyer, Paper
Adventures, Provo Craft)
Ribbon (Anna Griffin)
⅛" hole punch
Eyelets (Emagination Crafts)
Hammer
Eyelet-setting tools

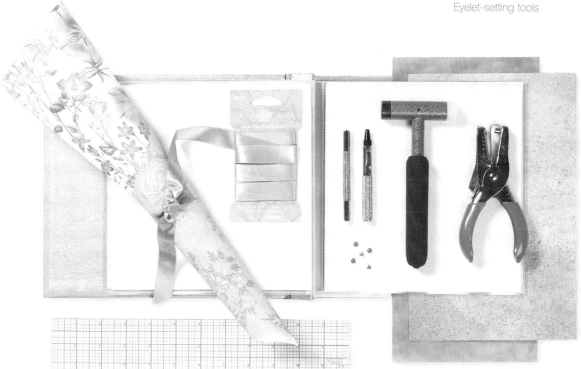

1 Double mat the opening photo on decorative papers. Punch two holes ½" down and 1" apart at the top of the mat.

Journaling tip

Find information on the Internet or cards that highlight special years, including important history and prices from that year. When interviewing a subject for stories and information, use various books that contain interview questions. They can be found in the library, bookstores or on the Internet.

3 Cross ends of the ribbon behind the photo mat and pull ends back to the front through opposite holes and trim ends.

Shortcuts

Sometimes you can't complete an album all by yourself. Enlist a friend or family member to help you with the project.

When using computer journaling for your album, save all files until the project is complete. This saves time if anything needs to be changed.

2 To make a french knot, thread both ends of the ribbon through holes from the front, with both ends extending out the back.

Other album ideas

FRIENDSHIP

Preserve memories of a friendship that has lasted over the years.

LETTERS

Make a title page featuring a photo of someone who has corresponded with you throughout the years. Fill the album with the cherished letters.

CAREER

A good gift to give upon retirement. Chronologically document a job, accomplishments and daily routine. Include photos of recipient and congratulations or memories from co-workers.

SCHOOL PORTRAITS

A quick album to create and a great gift for the graduate or parents of a graduate. Use one spread for each portrait.

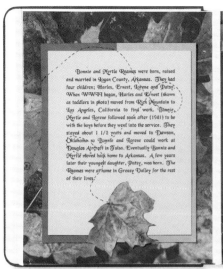

Record a family's history

Peggy has completed several cherished albums documenting her family's history. In this album she scanned and enlarged photos to create a focal point. Keep each spread tied together by using matching products. Simply mat photo and journaling and adhere to page. Journal an overview of the family history. This gift can be given several times by photocopying it for family members.

Album: Peggy Adair

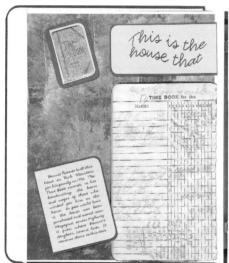

Watch a birthday girl grow up

Pick photos that show various stages of life to include in this album. Cut pages down so you can view all the photos together. Include a current photo. Create pages for guests to leave their birthday wishes.

Photos: Jill Neufeld

Calendar of events

CREATE A MEMORY OF YOUR FAMILY'S ACTIVITIES THROUGHOUT THE YEAR

It's easy to flip through a year of your family's life when you cut down album pages and record simple highlights each month. Several years of memories will fit into one small book, and getting into the habit of saving annual calendars will help you fill in the monthly details with ease.

Photos: Mary Ann Klassen

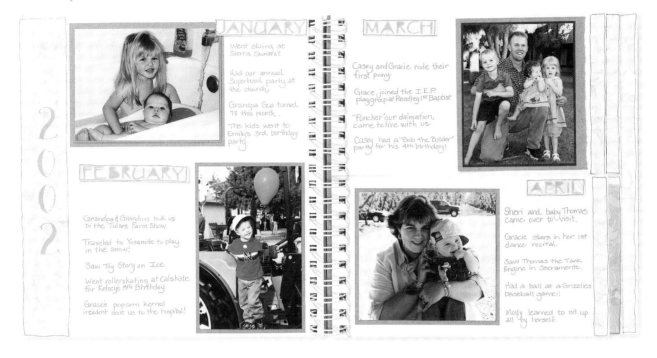

A *calendar-of-events album* records what happens through photos and journaling during a year, month or even a week. Keep a good record during the time frame that your album will cover for a very quick handmade gift. This type of album is a great way to use extra photos from throughout the year.

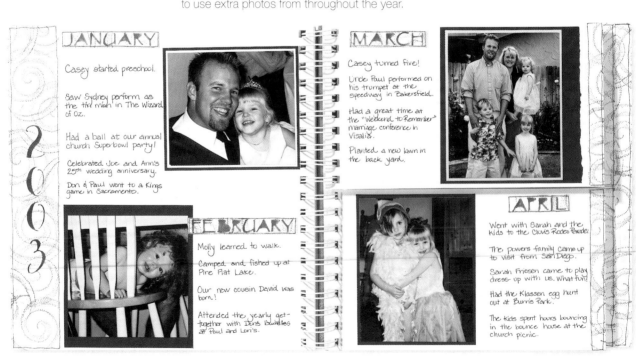

MAY

Had a Mother's Day Picnic with grandma at Woodward Park.

We threw Rachelle a beautiful bridal shower.

Monkeyed-around at the Chaffee Zoo.

Finished up our first year of Cubbies at church.

Georgie Lynn Meadors born May 22 to Paul & Lori.

JUNE

Aunt Rachelle got married!

Spent two days at Pismo Beach with the Stairs.

Took two weeks of swimming lessons at the Reedley pool.

Had a blast going to a week of vacation Bible School.

Casey graduated from Chapter One and Tristan graduated from 8th grade.

JULY

Went to the Ward's for our annual 4th of July barbecue.

Spent the weekend up at the cabin with Sarah, Jim, & the kids.

Had a blast at the Island Water Park with the Stairs.

Casey learned to swim!

Greg and Barb flew in from Canada for Don's 60th birthday.

Rented a houseboat and water-skiing at Pine Flat.

AUGUST

Gracie turns 4 years old!

Took a tour of the fire station. -got to spray the hose.

Casey started kindergarten at Washington elementary.

Spent the weekend up at Hartland for the Fall Festival.

Cooled off by floating down the Kings River.

Enjoyed a visit from Shari, Emily, and Andrew Allsup.

WHAT YOU'LL NEED

Album (Canson)

Metal straightedge ruler

Regular scissors

Journaling pens

Spiral stamp (Uptown Design)

Leaf stamp (Magenta)

Dye ink pads (Clearsnap)

Letter & number templates
(The Crafter's Workshop, Wordsworth)

Dragon clip (Dragon Ink)
with mini pompom for coloring

By cutting the pages of an 8½ x 11" album in half horizontally, each month can be showcased on its own half-page. This page design format makes it easy to identify the month of each year at a glance. If you are putting many years' of memories into one album, write the appropriate year after each month. Stamp the edges of the pages to help identify each new year with its own color. Use ink to fill in the template letters for a fast way to label each month.

Design tips

Save photo scraps. They can be used for punching interesting pieces to embellish a layout.

Use markers to get custom color on your stamp or to ink only parts of an image.

Shortcut

Journaling on vellum is simple when you slip a sheet of lined paper behind it to help line up your journaling.

1 Use paper and removable artist's tape ½" from edge of page to mask off part of the page for stamping. Stamp design.

2 With mask still applied, place template over stamped image and rub letters with pompom daubed in black ink.

3 Draw horizontal line half-way down across the page and cut on line to split page.

Other album ideas

SCHOOL YEAR

Showcase a child's accomplishments and growth during a school year. Include information about teachers and friends.

SPECIAL EVENTS

Help a loved one remember the year through the events he or she attended: movies, sports games, plays, programs. Add tickets, programs and other memorabilia.

YEAR OF DANCE

Create an album of the performances during an entire year. Include photos of practice, too.

CHILD TALK

Keep a journal handy to record interesting things your child says throughout the year. What a fun album to look back on.

4 To create tab cuts, draw vertical lines staggered ½" shorter than the previous one. Use scissors to cut the "stair-stepped" tabs.

Reflect on the past year at Christmas

Create a place to journal about highlights from the past year. Decorate tags with stamps and pop-dot accents and fibers. Add letter stickers. Use month stamps and highlight with white paper beneath vellum. Attach vellum with brad fasteners.

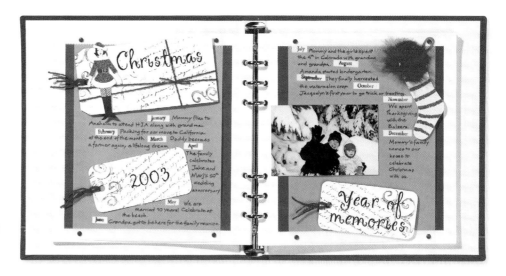

A child's year-in-review

Kristen took a picture of her daughter every week for her first year to create a beautiful keepsake and record of growth. Using precut papers from a pack helps make this a quick project. Crop and mount photos, add letter stickers and journaling.

Album: Kristen Jensen

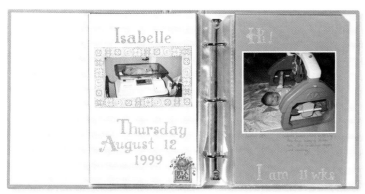

Journaling tip

Use a past year's calendar in an album. Cut it apart so that the activities that have been filled in become the journaling. Reduce each month to fit a page.

Season of sports

This album is a fun way to capture a single season. Create motion by punching squares that are cut consecutively smaller and mounted on a border. Use letter stickers on squares. Include practice photos and fund-raisers in the album.

Photos: MaryJo Regier

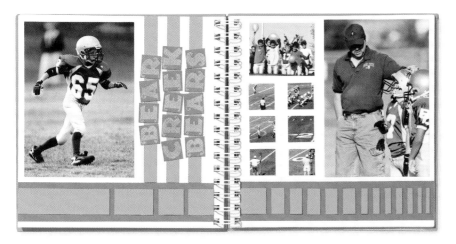

Tribute
CREATE A MEMORIAL FOR A LOVED ONE

Put together memories of a loved one quickly by using coordinating products from a single company. This book has a consistent flow and the decision of selecting product is simplified. Photocopy news clippings and obituary to include in the album. Highlight personal facts with computer journaling.

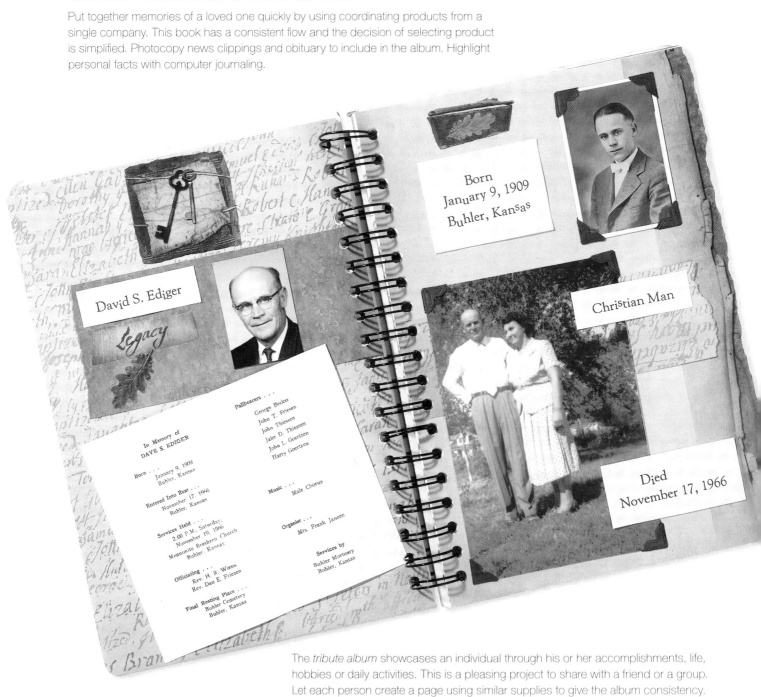

David S. Ediger

Legacy

Born
January 9, 1909
Buhler, Kansas

Christian Man

Died
November 17, 1966

In Memory of
DAVE S. EDIGER

Born . . . .
January 9, 1909
Buhler, Kansas

Entered Into Rest . . .
November 17, 1966
Buhler, Kansas

Services Held . . . .
2:00 P.M., Saturday,
November 19, 1966
Mennonite Brethren Church
Buhler, Kansas

Officiating . . . .
Rev. H. R. Wiens
Rev. Dan E. Friesen

Final Resting Place . . .
Buhler Cemetery
Buhler, Kansas

Pallbearers . . .
George Becker
John T. Friesen
John Thiessen
Jake D. Thiessen
John L. Goertzen
Harry Goertzen

Music . . .
Male Chorus

Organist . . .
Mrs. Frank Janzen

Services by
Buhler Mortuary
Buhler, Kansas

The *tribute album* showcases an individual through his or her accomplishments, life, hobbies or daily activities. This is a pleasing project to share with a friend or a group. Let each person create a page using similar supplies to give the album consistency.

Journaling tip

When writing someone's history, don't forget to answer the questions who, what, where, when and why to create a detailed album.

Punch holes in decorative background paper to cover each page completely. Tear strips of coordinating papers for each page. Add photos using photo corners. Punch the ends of the photocopied journaling to add into the binding. Embellish with coordinating stickers.

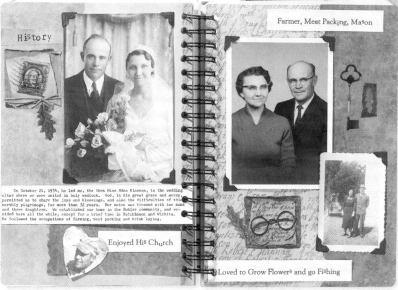

WHAT YOU'LL NEED

Album (Canson)

Coordinating paper and stickers
(Karen Foster Design)

Photo corners (Canson)

¼" hole punch (Fiskars)

Removable adhesive
(American Tombow)

Scissors

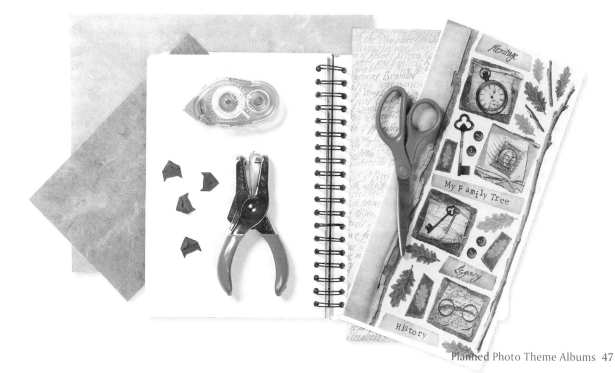

1 Tear a page out of the album to use as a pattern, apply removable adhesive to one side of the page. Adhere decorative paper to page lining up two edges.

Organizational tip

Plan before you begin your album. Almost everything takes longer if you don't lay out the album first.

Shortcuts

Using stickers and faux three-dimensional page accents saves time and keeps a small album from becoming too thick.

Use an album that is premade with decorative pages and add only photos and journaling.

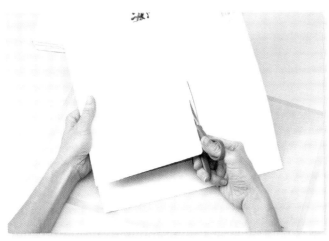

2 Trim remaining overhanging edges.

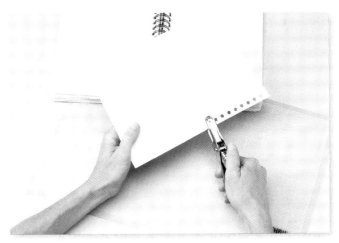

3 Line up punch with existing page holes and punch paper. Remove the pattern paper.

Other album ideas

FIRE OR POLICE STATION

Show appreciation for their hard work and service with newspaper clippings and notes of thanks.

ACKNOWLEDGE AN ACCOMPLISHMENT

Make an album to remember the presentation of an award. Journal about acts that led to the award.

INFLUENTIAL PERSON

Acknowledge someone who's been influential in your life: pastor, doctor or mentor.

4 Using scissors, clip the paper into each hole then push paper into binding, adhering to page beneath it. Use the same method to add journaling into binding.

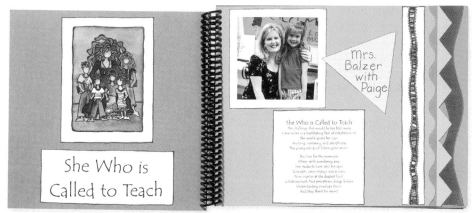

Students pay tribute to a teacher

Start with a fun, pre-designed album. Pick up design ideas from the style of the theme stickers. Repeat the wavy black lines by cutting each mat slightly wavy and rubbing the edges with a black ink pad. Continue this look throughout the entire album. Have each child write a note of thanks. Include photos of activities during the year.

Photos: Shelley Balzer

Thank a special coach

Duplicate the look of a team's logo and sports numbers in matching colors. Have each team member journal a note of thanks.

Photos: Kris Perkins

Random photo theme albums

A random photo theme album is also based upon a specific topic, but often uses unrelated, leftover or extra photos. Less time is spent in the organization process. These albums can be quite simple, only taking a few hours to complete. To create a successful album, gather photos that are best suited to your theme and continue a consistent design throughout the album.

One of the most fun aspects of creating this type of album is having the flexibility to showcase unrelated photos (photos taken at different times and on different rolls of film) in an emotionally or thematically related gallery. Random photos come together in harmony when used in ABC, Gardening, Advice, Words of Wisdom, Blessings, Pieces of Life and Storybook albums.

So think about an appropriate theme, gather those emotionally or thematically connected photos, and let the fun begin!

ABC

CREATE A FUN LEARNING TOOL FOR A CHILD

By using the same style of letters and border throughout this album, you create continuity even when the page themes are so varied. This is a good project to include the kids on. They love helping find the letter-related items.

Photos: Chelle Sugimoto

The *ABC album's* focus is each single letter of the alphabet. Decorate each page with the letter and related objects, words or photos. It's a unique teaching album for children, but can be used for many other topics—from a friendship album to a travel album.

Draw a simple border using a ruler to span the bottom of your page. Use one style of letter stickers and print words using a label maker for each page. Add photos, stickers and objects to correspond with each letter. Find or create texture on each page for the child to feel.

WHAT YOU'LL NEED

Album and page protectors (Mrs. Grossman's)

Mini cutting mat

Electronic labeling system (Brother P-Touch 1750)

Beads (Halcraft)

Flower punch (The Punch Bunch)

Stickers (Autumn Leaves, Creative Imaginations,
The Family Archives, Me & My Big Ideas,
Mrs. Grossman's, Sandylion)

3-D Keeper (3L)

Tacky tape (Art Accents)

Tape roller

Graphing ruler (C-Thru Ruler)

Scissors

Craft knife

Black journaling pen

1 Start at the right side of the sticker border. Using a ruler, draw border 1" inside the bottom of the page, ending at the sticker border. Outline the mat for the letter stickers with a marker and adhere to the bottom corner of the page.

Other album ideas

NUMBERS AND COLORS

Help a child learn to count or identify colors by filling this album with fun things he or she recognizes.

FAITH

Document a family's important beliefs or religious events and milestones.

WEDDING

A fun twist on a traditional wedding album. Add words like leap, faint and blue.

THANKFULNESS

Create an album showing what a family is thankful for, or reasons you are thankful for a specific person.

2 Silhouette cut photos and mount on mats, hand drawing a border. Add matted stickers and die cut.

3 Adhere tacky tape to page and apply small glass beads for texture.

Organization tip

While planning this album, keep a file folder or zippered sandwich bag handy. When you find a photo, object or sticker that corresponds with a letter, simply slip it in your folder. You can have several ongoing albums in various themes. When each folder or bag fills, complete the album and you'll have another special gift to give.

Journaling tip

When you have a new baby, create an ABC album. Using each letter of the alphabet, write about your hopes, dreams and aspirations for your child. Put these in an envelope on each page and give this gift when he or she is an adolescent.

4 Put the page into a page protector and mark placement of the beads with a marker. Removing page, slide a small cutting mat into the page protector and cut opening with a craft knife. Add related words to the bottom of the page with a label maker.

Give a gift of love

Use a letter of the alphabet to express your feelings. Stamp background pages in various colors. Punch a tag for each letter. Stamp and emboss the letter and tag. Attach small tag to vellum envelope with a brad fastener. Journal on large tag and slip it in the envelope. Embellish with 3-D stickers.

Photos: Nicole LaCour

Remember a child's words

Donna created a fun book for her son, Jared, by stamping his pronunciation of words on small mats. Match those words with stickers and use bright cardstock and patterned papers for the background.

Album: Donna Dresp

Shortcuts

Use only one word or letter with one photo per page in an ABC album. Lists of ABC words are easy to find in magazines and on the Internet. Many title ideas are also available.

Personalize a gardener's album

Include photos of the gardener's own flowers and quotes about the hobby he or she loves. Using a small square ink pad, stamp a background pattern on the page. Print journaling on vellum, printing the first letter of your alphabet word separately. Punch out letter and adhere to vellum tag. Add with a twist of paper fiber. Attach journaling to page with snaps; use similar placement of journaling on the back of each page to secure both at once.

Photo: Richard Gerbrandt

Advice or words of wisdom

TWENTY REASONS LIFE IS GOOD

This idea, inspired by Franci Kettman, reminds us of the important things in life. Choose twenty photos that have importance and print the journaling that inspired those choices. Surround the photos and journaling with matching stickers to create a consistent look.

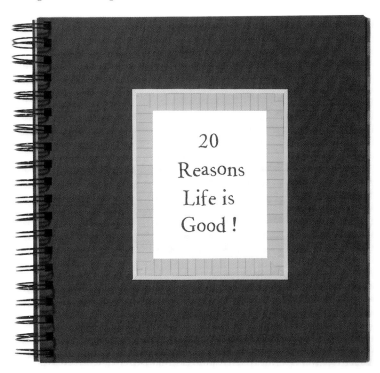

The focus in an album of *advice or words of wisdom* is the journaling. The words are often supported by photos that match the subject. Keep it simple and use the same design through the entire album. Focus on the journaling.

Pick background papers to coordinate with your photos and stickers. After adhering the background and journaling block to the page, cut strips of stickers so they are easier to manage. Lay border stickers around the edges. For a clean and finished look, miter the corners of each row of stickers. Add flower stickers for a final decoration.

Album (Canson)

Paper (Karen Foster Design, Magenta)

Border stickers (Mrs. Grossman's)

Flower stickers (Me & My Big Ideas)

Scissors

Tweezers

1 Cut sticker borders into strips long enough to cross at the corners. Lay the sticker border down, overlapping corners. Press to adhere centers, leaving corners loose.

Other album ideas

TEACHING ALBUM

Document how Grandma makes her special bread. Include pictures and the recipe.

RELIGION

Share information about beliefs and values related to a religion.

FAMILY TRADITION

Tell about the things a family does every year that has become their tradition.

ADVICE

Give a young person words of wisdom that can help and inspire.

Journaling tip

Using action words (verbs) and descriptive words (adjectives) in your journaling makes your messages more creative and entertaining. Collect quotes, poems and sayings to have on hand when you're ready to begin a project.

Design tip

Make sure there is no glue or tape showing on the finished album; it looks messy.

2 To make a "mitered" cut without a craft knife and ruler, line up scissor blades across the corner of the stickers where they cross. Cut through at the points that the stickers meet.

Shortcuts

Keep a journal at your bedside to jot down ideas; it's a great tool when you begin a project.

Using a template and marker is a quick way to get the look of a brad or eyelet, instead of the work and bulk of a real one.

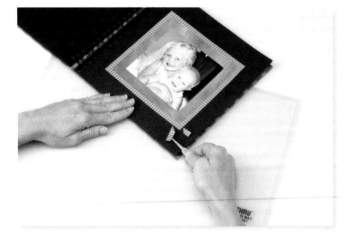

3 Remove the two cut-off ends with tweezers.

Inspire with quotes

This bedside album is filled with quotes to start each day. Select four colors of paper to use throughout the album. Mount butterfly stickers and small mat for word sticker. Draw tiny brad fasteners on title. Use quote stickers and draw borders around quotes for a finished look.

Wisdom for the groom

A fun little pocket-sized album filled with well-meaning advice from family and friends for a new husband is sure to be a hit! Adhere one strip of torn, patterned paper to each album page. Add cropped photos, mounted in photo corners, to all left pages. Adhere inked and ribbon-wrapped mini envelopes to all right pages. Finish by tucking journaled vellum tidbits of advice opposite each writer's photo.

Photos: Michele Gerbrandt

Flowers and verse

This accordion album is perfect to open and display so that the verse that runs throughout can be enjoyed. Back entire album with decorative paper, punch holes in background to tie photos into album with paper fiber. This allows you to hold photos on both sides of the page. Attach journaling block on torn mulberry. Journal with a template and two colors of watercolor pencils, then write over the word with a water brush to soften it.

Favorite photos

CREATE A BOOK OF TREASURED PHOTOS

In a beautiful book dedicated to her children, Debi has used the pictures themselves for continuity. After gathering favorite photos—some that had turned orange with age—she scanned them into her computer. Using software, Debi enlarged, repaired and printed the photos all in black-and-white. Each spread was decorated differently, but the same format was used throughout.

Album: Debi Boring

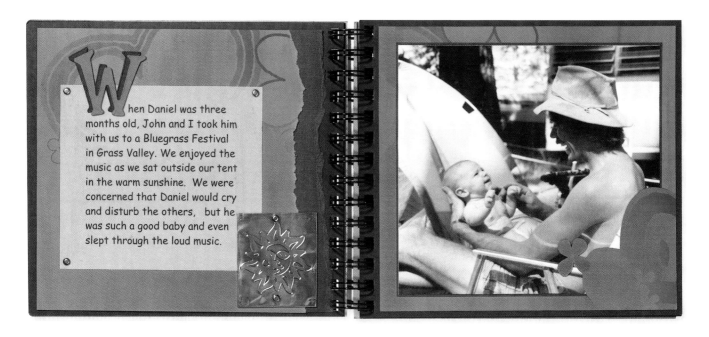

When Daniel was three months old, John and I took him with us to a Bluegrass Festival in Grass Valley. We enjoyed the music as we sat outside our tent in the warm sunshine. We were concerned that Daniel would cry and disturb the others, but he was such a good baby and even slept through the loud music.

The *favorite photos album* is made up of photos that have no specific connection but are brought together for a simple theme and for the simple reason that they are truly cherished. These albums are often titled with a single sentiment, such as Joy, Inspire or Laugh. Select the theme of your album and then find random photos to represent that theme.

Happy Birthy dear Kimmee..... Kimberlee was NOT happy when we started singing Happy Birthday to her at her second birthday party. She did not like the attention, and she began to cry. I had to ask her guests to move away from her, so she would settle down. She was a very shy little girl.

Found this cute little tricycle for two at a second hand store called Trader Tots. I always intended to paint it red, but they grew out of it before I got around to it. Daniel would peddle Kimmee around in it at our house on Mello Ln. (Kimmee's holding her Chuck E. Cheese mouse and wearing her hat that eventually became covered with pins)

Have some fun designing different looks for each spread using 3-D stickers, eyelets and brad fasteners. Print computer journaling on paper and tear around it to fit on page. Mat on background paper; repeat. Tear ends of coordinating paper on opposite page. Continue the consistency by repeating the drop shadow on a die-cut letter.

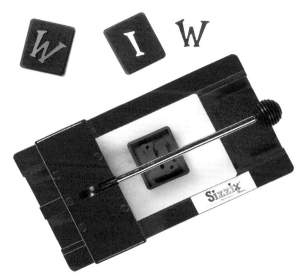

WHAT YOU'LL NEED

Album (Running Rhino & Co.)
Paper (Club Scrap)
Die-cut letters (Sizzix/Provo Craft)
Stickers (EK Success)
Embossed copper (Global Solutions)
Brad fasteners (Creative Impressions)
Removable adhesive
(American Tombow)
Scissors
Craft knife

Other album ideas

RELAXATION

An enjoyable album to pull out on a stressful day. Fill with photos of things that make you feel relaxed and words of reflection.

DREAMS FOR MY FAMILY

Journal about your aspirations for family members. Include favorite photos.

FAVORITE THINGS

Fill this album with photos of all the things that someone loves.

CELEBRATION OF LIFE

Share with someone the many things that make life a celebration.

1 Scan old photos on a computer scanner. Adjust size, repair scratches and convert to black-and-white using photo-editing software program or photo-duplication machine. Print all of the photos the same size for continuity and crop to fit album page.

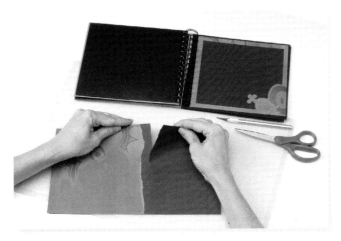

Shortcuts

Know your work habits; if you like to spread material out as you work, start with enough workspace—such as a long countertop or large table.

2 Trim two sheets of complementary-colored cardstock to fit page, allowing for a small border of page to show. Tear edges of cardstock and mount on page.

Journaling tip

Using a classic font throughout your album gives a formal look. Varying different sizes and weights of the same font throughout your album will create a more casual, playful look.

Organization tip

Organize photos and negatives in photosafe storage boxes so they are easy to access for quick projects.

3 Create die-cut letter from decorative paper using a Sizzix die-cutting machine. Cut a second letter from black paper. Mount top letter slightly lower and to the right of the black letter to create a drop shadow.

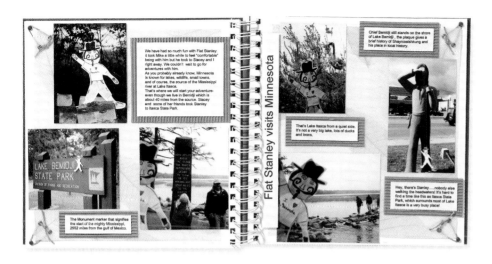

Travel without leaving home

A switch on the same theme, these photos are all of one subject but come from random places. Create a spread for each location your Flat Stanley travels. Back the page with vellum. Tie at corners with a brad, eyelets and jute. Add computer journaling to corrugated mats.

Photos: Mike Haugen

Blessings to remember

Joy created a book of things that were special in her life as a gift to herself. She decorated the handmade accordion-fold album with handmade and decorative papers. Collage a page with a music sheet. Tear papers to become journaling mats. Add stickers for journaling and decoration.

Album: Joy Candrian

Gather pieces of life

Choose photos that contain everyday items (small-scale images work best). Using different-sized square punches, punch out interesting details. Fit photos randomly in an accordion album. Add sticker journaling on premade envelopes and tags. Embellish with mosaic stickers.

Storybook
CAST A CHILD AS THE MAIN CHARACTER

Give a world of imagination to a child by placing him or her in a well-loved story. Take pictures of your child in poses that re-enact the storyline you choose. Use the photos along with the text of the story on your pages.

The *storybook album* puts a child inside his or her own story and gives the child a sense of pride. Start with a well-loved story that can be journaled easily in the pages of an album. Add photos of the child that relate to the storyline. This album can be illustrated with art similar to the book or make up and illustrate a story with the child's personality in mind.

It followed her to school one day, which was against the rules.

WHAT YOU'LL NEED

Album (Mrs. Grossman's)

Paper (K & Co.)

Calligraphy pen (Staedtler)

Letter stickers (EK Success)

Lamb stickers
(Me & My Big Ideas, Paper Adventures, PSX Design)

¾" and ⅝" square punches
(Emagination Crafts, The Punch Bunch)

Adhesive application machine (Xyron)

Photo splits

Pencil

Scissors

Craft knife

Using preprinted paper makes this album come together quickly. Trim down papers to fit the album pages. Silhouette cut the photos of your child, then turn them into stickers using a Xyron™ adhesive-application machine. Work with the layout until you can fit the story and photos on the page. Adhere the photos then handwrite the story, creating illuminated letters to begin each phrase.

1 Cut a window the size of your album page. To determine the part of the paper you want to use, move the window around on top of your decorative paper to isolate the imagery you want to use. Then use the window to outline your paper to cut to the size of your page.

Shortcuts

Save time-consuming artistic designs for the title page or album cover.

Give a mat an aged look by chalking the edges.

Before stitching cardstock, punch your pattern with a 1/16" hole punch.

Photo tip

For a more pleasing scenic shot, place or capture the horizon in the top or bottom one-third of your photo. When photographing a child, kneel down to get on the child's level. If taken from above, the child appears distorted.

2 Use scissors to silhouette cut the child from the photos, cutting with a craft knife in tiny areas. Use a Xyron adhesive-application machine to make the photo into a sticker and adhere it to the page.

3 Punch a 3/4" purple square and top with a 5/8" yellow square, adhere a letter sticker on top to create an illuminated letter. Hand journal the remaining story across the page.

Other album ideas

POEM

Journal a poem in an album and add photos that illustrate the topic.

ANIMAL STORY

Use a pet as the inspiration for a storyline.

FAVORITE SONG

Use the lines from a child's favorite song to run through the album.

PERSONAL STORY

Help your child visualize a friend or family member by putting his or her life in story form.

Create a fantasy world

In an album for her son, Becky turned him into imaginary characters. Change a color photo to sepia-tone on a photo duplication machine; chalk and mat. Highlight words in the journaling by drawing a box around them. Use outlines for quick-finish designs.

Album: Becky Baack

Personalize a comic book

Use random photos to illustrate a handdrawn comic book—an idea sure to be a funny favorite. Put some favorite silhouette-cropped photos into an album. Draw cartoons of other family members or friends in watercolor pencils. Add punched cartoon bubbles and journaling to illustrate the story.

Album: Pennie Stutzman

Stitch together nursery rhymes

Using costumes and stitching, Shannon made her son a book of nursery rhymes. Print the rhyme on primary-colored cardstock. To quickly stitch borders with needle and embroidery floss, use a paper that has a cutting grid preprinted on the backside. Stamp the title.

Album: Shannon Taylor

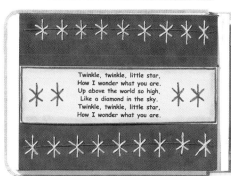

Tribute

SEND LOVE TO GRANDPARENTS

Complete an album quickly and inexpensively by decorating the pages with only pen work. Susan drew simple flowers, dots and leaves to add design to this album. No extra papers are needed and you can personalize the colors. Verse or quotes matching the theme of the album becomes the journaling.

Album: Susan McFall

With each birth, a new grandparent is born

When we hold a baby in our arms, we borrow a precious gift from God

All that is beautiful can be found in Grandma's heart

Loveable, Snuggable Hugs to You

The *tribute album* is a theme album designed to honor or give thanks to a certain individual or group. As with the *miscellaneous album*, this album could be about any number of subjects, the main consideration being the recipient. You want to create an album in a subject that will surprise and delight the recipient. Consider a gift for an elderly person in assisted-care living. Create a gift of memories for him or her to share with others. Turn each page of a small, spiral album into a coupon book of special favors you can do for another. Or feature 25 reasons your child is the most special kid in the world. This may not be as simple, but the gift of self-esteem is invaluable.

Lay out your photos and journaling first in this album. Fill in the extra spaces with hand-drawn designs. Change designs from page to page, but keep the basic theme and color scheme for a consistent look throughout the album.

WHAT YOU'LL NEED

Album (Close To My Heart)

Dottariffic journaling pens
(EK Success)

Fine-tip journaling pen (Sakura)

Pencil with eraser

Photo tips

To get the best detail and expressions in your photos, get closer to your subject. Focus in on just the face.

Organization tip

When you get photos processed, take the time to jot down any information while it is still fresh in your mind. Your notes will spark memories that will make it easier to journal about later.

Design tip

When your creativity is lagging, change your scene. Take a walk outside. Become inspired by everyday things.

1 Draw the outlines of a flower with a pencil and trace inside the outline with the thick end of the pink marker, filling in the center of the flower.

2 Fill in the petals with the fine tip of the purple pen.

3 Using a fine-tip black marker, outline the flower petals and center, adding swirls to the edges. Add dots and border lines.

Other album ideas

TEN THINGS THAT MAKE YOU SPECIAL

Create a gift to give to a friend, spouse, parent or child, listing his or her special traits.

ANNIVERSARY

Say "I love you" with an album of love notes and quotes.

FAREWELL

Make a farewell album for a co-worker leaving a job or a neighbor moving away. Fill this album with memories he or she can take along.

4 Add dots with the small end of the pen. Make simple flowers by dotting with the large end of the marker and adding petals with the fine-tipped pen.

A birthday gift for a friend

Julie made this birthday gift by e-mailing her friend a questionnaire to fill in. With the information and a roll of film taken especially for this album, she personalized a special gift. Cover pages with decorative paper. Print journalling on vellum and adhere to page with adhesive. Handcut fun letters and adhere. Silhouette-crop photos in unique layout to express the personality.

Album: Julie Labuszewski

Special Father's Day gift

Becky's annual Father's Day gift project is a handmade album for her son Nic to give to his father. Hand journal a title page and attach with brad fasteners to cardstock that has been sanded for an aged look. Trace your child's hand. Journal about what he likes about his dad. Include pages with current photos and interesting ones from that year.

Album: Becky Baack

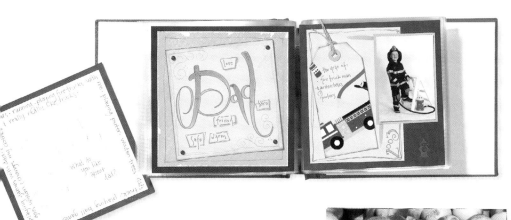

Saying thanks for a memory

Use photos taken on a trip or vacation to say "thank you" to your host or hostess. Scan and print a photo in sepia-tone to use as background paper. Color in lettering template with chalks, using different shades. Mount photos and journal with template.

CHAPTER 4
Specialty albums

Its physical shape defines the specialty album. It may be small or even miniature in size. Pages may flip up, unlike a standard page-turning album. A specialty album may be housed in a box or featured on a tag. It can also be miniature and worn around the neck. This type of album is a quick project that makes a fresh and innovative gift. Maintain a consistent design throughout for continuity and to keep assembly almost effortless.

Use your theme to help determine the shape and style of an album to custom-fit your project. Here's where shape templates, dies and jumbo punches can come in handy; use them to create the cover and pages of a miniature gift album.

Again, begin with a theme and gather photos. Then get creative with bindings. And save small tins, too. Nothing's off limits!

Brag book
CREATE A BRAG BOOK FOR GRANDMA

Personalize this album by making it yourself. Pick the paper that best suits your theme, then stamp the pattern. Cut it out and glue it together. It takes only a short time to decorate and complete these small pages.

The *brag book* is a theme album giving the creator a place to display his or her most precious photos, memorabilia or journaling. These albums are meant to be carried with you and displayed at any given opportunity. There are many patterns and templates available to help you create these small albums.

WHAT YOU'LL NEED

Album stamps (Limited Edition Rubberstamps)

Paper (Paper Adventures)

Ribbon (Robin's Nest)

Beads (Hot Off The Press)

Black ink pad (Clearsnap)

Liquid glue (American Tombow)

Metal straightedge ruler

Craft knife

Scissors

Embossing stylus

Make pages from paper that coordinates with the cover. Give this album variety by choosing a pattern with pages that have openings for photos, pocket pages or envelope pages. Three stamped pages are recommended for this album, creating a six-page album when finished. Before gluing pages into the album, add ribbon and beads for decoration.

Photo tips

Cut apart the index prints from a developed roll of film to fill a small album.

Take photos farther away from your subject; when cropped, these will fit on a small pad.

1 Stamp the cover and page patterns on the wrong side of coordinating papers.

2 Line up ruler on broken lines and score with a stylus. Cut out pattern pieces, cutting center window openings with a craft knife. Fold flaps.

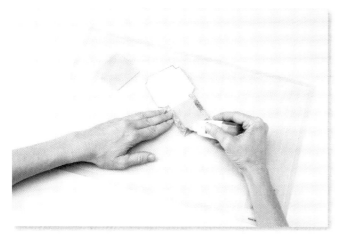

3 Glue two pieces of 2⅜" square cardboard inside front cover, leaving the center uncovered to become the book's spine. Glue flaps over cardboard and center flaps to cover.

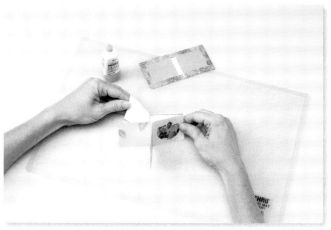

4 Crop and glue photos in place behind the window page. Put pages in order, gluing back to back. Leave front and back unglued; they will be glued into the spine.

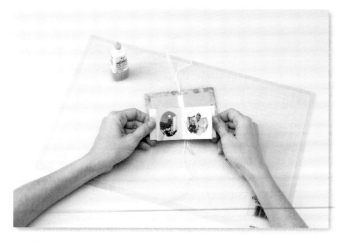

5 Glue string of beads and ribbon in the spine. Glue front and back pages inside the cover, centering pages.

Shortcuts

Join friends to make these albums assembly-line style so everyone has one to take home and fill.

Use square punches to cut photos and mats to fit this miniature album.

Other album ideas

PET ALBUM

Show off a pet that is an important part of your life.

PARTY CRAFT

A great craft for kids to make at parties and fill with photos of their friends.

HERITAGE

Use copies of your old photos to show your heritage.

BIRTH ANNOUNCEMENT

A great way to show off a new baby. Include weight, length and birth date.

INSPIRATION

Fill this little album with quotes, verses and photos that inspire you throughout the day.

Create a key chain of precious photos

Simply cut small pages of cardstock and add your photos, journaling and any flat embellishments. Use a Xyron adhesive-application machine or copy center to laminate the pages. Set an eyelet at the top of each page to hang on the key chain. By putting an elastic band through the center of the cover, you can hold all the pages together when album is closed.

Photos: Elizabeth Friesen

Design tip

Use tiny tools and supplies to decorate small albums. A tiny punch, letter stickers, stencils, stamps and fine-tipped pens work well to add tiny details.

Flip calendars

FLIP THROUGH A CALENDAR YEAR OF MEMORIES

Use a large stamp to quickly create a 52-page week-at-a-glance calendar. The design of the stamp gives the album consistency. Change the colors to identify each month. Add ribbons to the bottom of the front and back covers. When the calendar is open and the ribbons tied underneath, it creates its own stand.

Photos: Kris Perkins

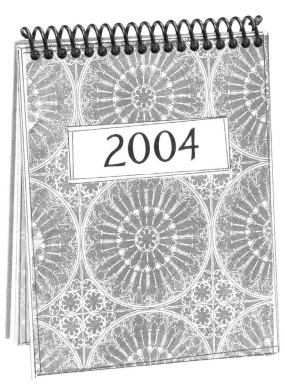

The *flip calendar* is a useful gift that reveals precious memories all year long. Each page can be designed to cover a calendar week, or use an annual calendar and change the quote each week. For a speedier version, create one page for each month. Personalize your calendar by including holidays, birthdays and anniversaries. Give yourself plenty of time to complete this gift before New Year's.

Several large stamps are designed to fit the size of a card. Hobby stores carry precut paper in card size or cut pages to fit the stamp. Stamp background on pages, masking for the placement of the month and date. Finish edges with a ruler and pen lines and repeat around masked area. Stamp dates with magnetic date stamp. Change color for special dates: anniversary, holidays and birthdays. Make front and back cover from chipboard adding ribbons for the stand. Have the cover and pages bound together at a copy center.

WHAT YOU'LL NEED

Album (handmade)

Stamp (Close To My Heart)

Colorbox ink pads (Clearsnap)

Magnetic date stamps (Making Memories)

Sticky notes

Brayer

Craft knife

Metal straightedge ruler

Black journaling pen

1 Use a sticky note to mask each calendar page in the same place.

2 Ink the stamp and leave the wet stamp design upright. Place masked side of page on inked surface of stamp and rub entire surface of stamp with brayer or other firm surface.

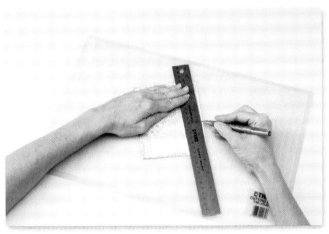

3 Remove mask and draw lines with pen and ruler. Stamp dates.

4 Adhere ribbon between the front and back pages and the chipboard to create a cover and stand. Have the album comb-bound at a copy center.

Other album ideas

SCHOOL YEAR CALENDAR

Using the school's schedule, create a calendar for your child, highlighting holidays and special events.

SPORTS SEASONS

Make your child or husband a sports calendar to help him or her remember practice schedules and game dates.

VERSE OF THE WEEK

Fill this calendar with a seasonally appropriate verse for each week or month of the year.

GIFT FOR THE JOURNALER

Create a calendar with spaces each day of the week large enough for a journaler to fill in the day's events. This album becomes a memory of your year.

Quote for the week

Using a larger format flip book, attach a tear-off calendar to the bottom half of the back cover. Cut the remaining pages short. Decorate each page, adding a quote or saying. Layer cut and torn printed paper over cardstock. Tear and distress with sandpaper. Attach with paper strip and eyelets. Highlight preprinted vellum quote by backing with white paper.

Collage an artistic calendar

Create a gift without searching for photos. The design itself becomes a piece of art. Adhere a page from an old book, vellum and decorative paper to the page. Add floral stickers with self-adhesive foam spacers for a focal point with depth. Stamp the day and date. Personalize this calendar by subject: perhaps fishing for Grandpa, a sewing theme for Mom or a girlish theme for a teenage daughter or niece.

Organization tip

When you have a deadline for your gift, use a planner to record ideas. It can be an invaluable tool in the developing stage. Make a list of the products you'll need, gather journaling and quotes so it will all be in one place when you start to assemble your album.

Design tip

Create a page about the author to include with your gift. Give information about yourself and your reasons for creating the gift.

Shortcuts

Collect sayings from cards, calendars and books to have on hand when starting a project. Before binding a calendar, make photocopies on good cardstock and send this gift to several people. Print a free calendar from the Internet to use on your project.

Cards

CONVERT AN ACCORDION CARD

Make a quick and easy photo gift out of a card. Crop an accordion-fold card into an elongated triangle to create an interesting closure. Stamp along edges that will be seen when the card is closed. Slice a panoramic photo and adhere into card. Journal a sentiment. Run a pen along the edges; close the card and stamp the front.

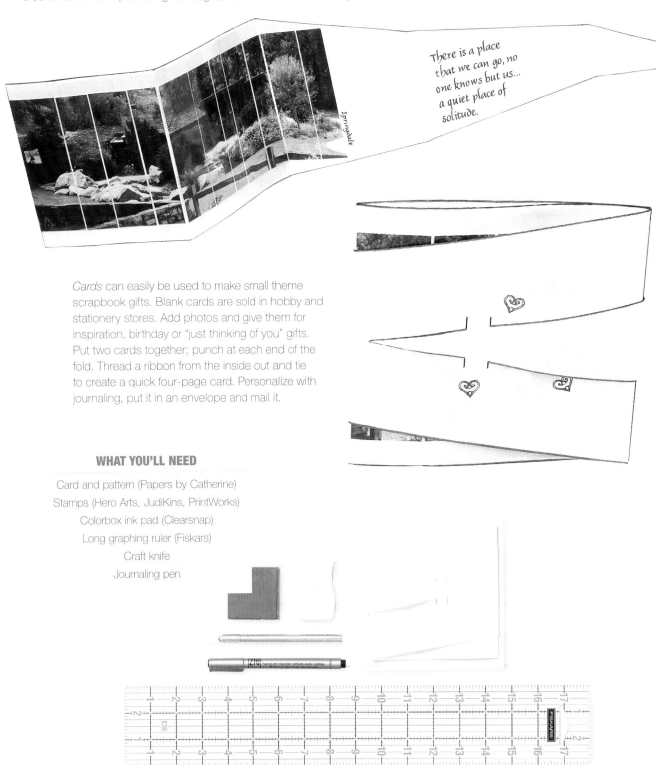

There is a place that we can go, no one knows but us... a quiet place of solitude.

Cards can easily be used to make small theme scrapbook gifts. Blank cards are sold in hobby and stationery stores. Add photos and give them for inspiration, birthday or "just thinking of you" gifts. Put two cards together; punch at each end of the fold. Thread a ribbon from the inside out and tie to create a quick four-page card. Personalize with journaling, put it in an envelope and mail it.

WHAT YOU'LL NEED

Card and pattern (Papers by Catherine)

Stamps (Hero Arts, JudiKins, PrintWorks)

Colorbox ink pad (Clearsnap)

Long graphing ruler (Fiskars)

Craft knife

Journaling pen

1 See illustration that came with the card. Draw lines from top of the third panel to the middle at the end of the card. Center two parallel lines 2" from the right side of the third panel, ⅜" apart and 1" tall.

2 Cut along angled lines, trimming off pen marks. Cut slits on interior lines to create slots.

3 Decorate along the edges of card with shadow stamps. Close the card and stamp the front with decorative stamps.

Envelopes & tags
TREASURES INSIDE AN ENVELOPE

Create an album that you can tuck keepsake photos and memorabilia into. This *envelope album* has an artsy, handmade look to it. Tear the ends off of small mailer envelopes. Use chalks to color the fronts of each envelope. Stamp randomly and decorate the front. Have the envelopes bound together at a copy center. Try creating a sewing theme by stitching on envelopes and decorating with a needle and thread on the front. Or, perhaps, try a gardening theme by filling with seed packets and photos of flowers. Another option: Preserve holiday memories in this type of album. Create the album without tearing the ends off the envelopes to keep memorabilia enclosed.

Photos: Kelli Noto

WHAT YOU'LL NEED

Envelopes (DMD)

Chalk (Stampin' Up!)

Chalk enhancer
(Craft-T)

Sponge-tip applicators

Journaled block (Daisy D's)

Tags (7 Gypsies)

Skeletonized leaves
(Graphic Products)

Word sticker (Bo-Bunny Press)

Gold leaf (Graphic Products)

Netting (Magenta)

Stamp (JudiKins)

Buttons and feather (found)

Circle cutter

Ribbon

1 Tear ends of envelopes, staggering lengths.

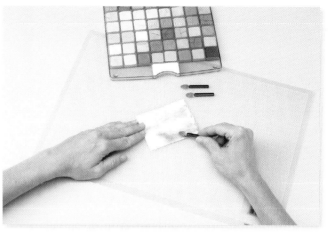

2 Rub chalks on envelopes with sponge applicator.

3 Blend chalk colors with chalk enhancer, rubbing in a circular motion. Allow to dry.

4 Stamp envelopes. Add word sticker, buttons and feather. Fill envelopes with treasures. Have envelopes bound together at copy center.

Put your memories on a tag

Creating a small *tag album* for a special gift is fun and simple. To bind it together, just run a string or ribbon through the holes and add beads and charms to the ends. There are many styles of tags available. Punches and templates will allow you to pick your own cardstock for the tags. Create a little album of love: Leave your lip print on a tag for your sweetheart, something you value in life for your kids or twelve reasons why a person is a favorite teacher. Dye tags with walnut ink. Adhere vellum and photos behind precut openings. Stamp dates on vellum and add stickers.

Albums in a box

COFFEE TABLE ALBUM IN A BOX

Decorate a CD tin; it's the perfect size to hold a string of 3 x 5½" photos. Covering the entire top of the tin with a sheet of tacky tape makes this a unique and easy project. Decorate lid with tiles and beads. Title with sticker letters. Make a chain of photos with jump rings. Use mint tins to hold cropped or wallet-sized photos. Try decorating a tin to hold an album of a date to the prom and include dried petals from the corsage. Use this idea to preserve a vacation at the beach and decorate the tin with shells and sand. Display your album for all to enjoy.

Photos: Amy Horn

WHAT YOU'LL NEED

CD-ROM tin

Tiles (Sweetwater)

Scrappy Sheet (Magic Scraps)

Paper (Mustard Moon)

Beads (JewelCraft, Provo Craft)

Tiny glass marbles (Halcraft)

Tray (Inkerbelle)

Letter stickers (Wordsworth)

Jump rings (Sulyn Industries)

Watercolor pens (EK Success)

⅛" hole punch (Fiskars)

Needle-nose pliers

1 Cover entire top of tin with a with a sheet of Scrappy Sheet adhesive trimmed to fit tin lid top. Remove cover of tape.

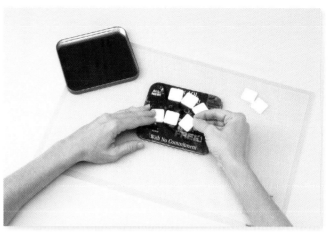

2 Adhere tiles to top of tin.

3 Pour beads onto the top of tin, covering as completely as possible; press. Pour tiny glass marbles into any remaining openings.

4 Color tiles with watercolor marker and smear with fingertip to blend. Apply letter stickers.

5 Mount quote onto paper inside the lid of the tin. Hold photos right-side together and punch ⅛" holes in four corners of photos. Chain photos together with jump rings.

Mini albums
CAPTURE A MINIATURE MEMORY

These *miniature scrapbooks* are meant to be decorated and filled with memories of a moment or sentiments to lift someone's spirit. They can be worn around your neck, hung on a rearview mirror or carried in your purse. Debra Glanz, owner of Reminiscence Papers, says, "They are meant to capture a moment, not to last for generations." Start with the color and style of album that will fit your theme. Personalize the cover, adding beads, charms, stickers, etc., then fill the pages. Polaroid I-Zone pictures fit perfectly in the mini album and are a fast way to capture a moment. Perhaps fill your mini album with phone numbers and pictures of each person or fill it with a book of poems. Use this type of album for a learning tool to teach a child about facial expressions by filling the album with photos of happy, sad, mad, scared and surprised expressions.

WHAT YOU'LL NEED

Albums (Creative Imaginations,
Reminiscence Papers)
I-Zone camera and film (Polaroid)
Sticker (Paper Adventures)
Tag (Avery)
Letter stamps (Hero Arts)
Word sticker (Bo-Bunny Press)
Tiny glass marbles and beads (Halcraft)
Flakes and tape (Magic Scraps)
Typewriter words (7 Gypsies)
Eyelet word, chain beads & shaped clips
(Making Memories)
Mulberry Paper (DMD)
Charms (source unknown)
Bradwear (Creative Imaginations)
Scissors
Adhesive (American Tombow)
Black journaling pen

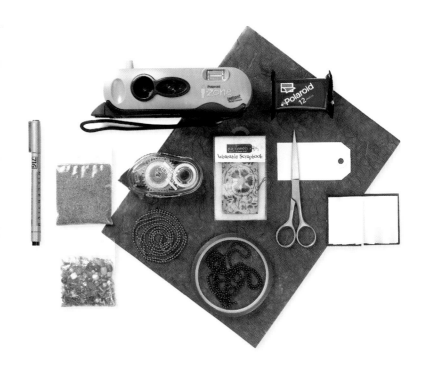

1 Take pictures at an event with the I-Zone camera. For best results, stand approximately 4' away from the subject when shooting. Vertical photos fit best in the tiny albums.

2 Crop photos on cutting lines and adhere in album.

3 Mount journaling blocks on mulberry paper romnants and tear around edges.

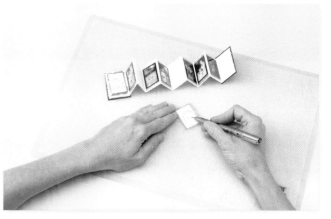

4 Journal in blank journaling blocks with a pen.

Altered books
SCRAPBOOKING BECOMES ART

Let the art represent the theme of your pictures. Fun and playful pictures of sisterly love are showcased by cutting a window in the pages and decorating with inks, stamps, decorative papers and stickers. Use similar materials and color scheme throughout the album for a harmonious look.

Photos: Susan McFall

Journaling tips

If you have no room for journaling on your page, create a pocket behind a photo to slip the journ-aling into.

Journal an album in the voice of a child.

The *altered book* is used to let your creativity show through. Begin with an old used book. Estimate how many pages your book will need to have. Pick the most interesting pages you want to show for illustrations, phrases or titles. Glue groups of pages together, leaving the interesting pages showing. A book of 200 pages can become a book of 10 pages with ease. Use your scrapbooking supplies to add artistic decoration. It's the perfect place to experiment with new ideas. Add photos and journaling and your old book becomes a cherished new album.

Packs of collage papers make design decisions much easier. Interesting papers, tags and artwork are combined in these packs to inspire artistic experimentation. Glue groups of pages together using wood glue to prevent pages from warping. Clamp each section while drying. Dry thoroughly before decorating. Cut a window in your book to display two photos at once. Use the illustrations and special phrases in the book to help determine the placement of photos and decorative elements. After gluing papers around photos and openings, add decorative elements until you have a balanced design. Hand-letter additional journaling and add stamping ink.

WHAT YOU'LL NEED

Album (antique book)

Collage paper (Books By Hand, DMD)

Vellum paper (DMD)

Stickers (K & Co., Making Memories, NRN Designs)

Netting (Magenta)

Liquid adhesive (Hot Off The Press)

Scissors

Craft knife

Brown ink pad (Clearsnap)

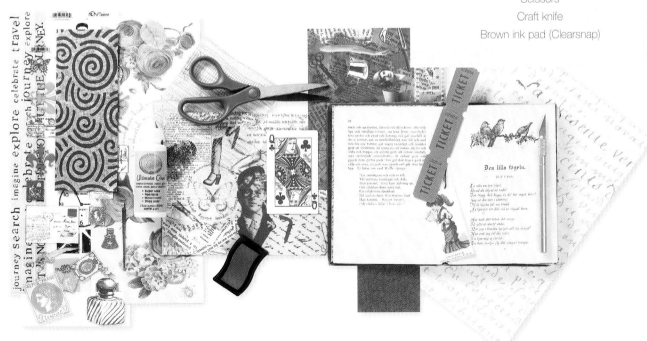

1 Glue groups of pages together, separate openings and let dry thoroughly.

2 Cut out a window in the center of the page with a craft knife. Position photos in the windows and crop them to reveal the book's illustrations.

3 Begin layering decorative papers and stickers to fit around photos and their openings, tearing random edges to create interest. Add materials until you create a pleasing balance.

4 Rub an inkpad over sections of papers and stickers to create an aged look. Finish album by adding handwritten journaling.

Other album ideas

CHILD'S PERSPECTIVE OF LIFE

Fill an album with carefree, sunny days and his or her best friend, teddy bear.

TEEN'S LIFE

Pick favorite colors and fill with images that surround his or her days.

MY THOUGHTS

Make a gift to yourself and include your personal philosophies, insights and mantras.

FAVORITE CELEBRITY

Fill with information, clippings and photos of someone's favorite idol.

Design tips

If you can't decide on colors for your project, use a big box of crayons and try a variety of color combinations.

Make sure your layout is not so cluttered that you can't see the photos. The photos and journaling should remain the focal point. Start with basic elements and add slowly until you have the perfect balance.

Shortcuts

To make cutout template letters quicker, draw the letter and cut loosely around the line. It's easier than following the lines exactly.

Instead of gluing together each page of an altered book, use eyelets or wire to hold groups of pages together.

Materials & credits

PAGE 3 BOOKPLATE

Album (DMD), Galaxy markers (American Crafts), Artwork: Susan McFall

PAGES 6-12 PEOPLE WHO LOVE ME

Album (Kolo); paper (Crafter's Workshop, Design Originals, Karen Foster Design, Paper Adventures, Scrap Ease); vellum paper (DMD); letter templates (EK Success, Wordsworth); ribbon, eyelets (Emagination Crafts), eyelet hole punch and setter (Making Memories), hammer

PAGE 11

"Becky" photo used with permission from Lifetouch Studios.

PAGE 14 ALBUM COVER

Album (Canson), paper (Design Originals), mulberry paper (DMD, PrintWorks), vellum paper (DMD), sticky-face stickers (Wish in the Wind), Polyflake (Glitterex Corp.), letter stickers (Wordsworth)

PAGE 19 SEASONS IN REVIEW

Album (Canson), paper (Design Originals), mulberry paper (DMD, PrintWorks), vellum paper (DMD), sticky-face stickers (Wish in the Wind), Polyflake (Glitterex Corp.)

PAGE 19 CALENDAR

Album (Canson), paper (Ellison, Provo Craft), stickers (EK Success), calendar (Limited Edition Rubberstamps). Calendar Art inspired by Judy Martin; Photo: Richard Gerbrandt

PAGE 23 WEDDING

Album (Bound + D/termined), paper (EK Success), flower stickers (Magenta), letter stickers (Colorbök), photo corners (Canson), Photo: Integrity Photography

PAGE 23 PARTY FAVOR

Album (DMD), stamp (Magenta), punch (Emagination Crafts), pens (EK Success)

PAGE 23 BABY SHOWER

Album (Kolo), collage papers (DMD), lettering template (Wordsworth), crystal rhinestones (JewelCraft), Photo: Susan Gerbrandt

PAGE 27 Q & A FOR GRANDPARENTS

Album (Running Rhino & Co.), paper (Hot Off The Press)

PAGE 27 FAMILY TREE

Album (DMD), paper (Anna Griffin), textured paper (Emagination Crafts), paper ribbon (Emagination Crafts), leaf punch (Family Treasures), ink (Clearsnap), ribbon

PAGE 31 GOALS & WISHES

Album (Mrs. Grossman's), paper (Scrappin' Dreams), stamps (Hero Arts, PSX Design), ink (Clearsnap), sticker eyelets (Mark Enterprises)

PAGE 31 AUTOGRAPH BOOK

Album (Mrs. Grossman's), paper (Hot Off The Press), die cuts (Paper Garden), Photo: Kris Perkins

PAGE 31 ADVICE

Album (C-Thru Ruler), paper (Provo Craft), letter stamps (Hero Arts), ink (Clearsnap), rectangle hand punch (Fiskars)

PAGE 32 ALBUM COVER

Album (Awesome Albums), paper (Autumn Leaves), sticker verse (Wordsworth), appliqué (Hirschberg Schutz & Co.), fibers

PAGE 37 NEW COUPLE

Album (DMD), lace paper (PrintWorks), mulberry paper (DMD, PrintWorks), skeletonized leaf (Graphic Products), letter stickers (EK Success), Photos: Angela Siemens, Manuel F. Sousa; Album: Angela Siemens

PAGE 37 TRIP

Album handmade with paper (Strathmore), Creamcoat paint (Delta), stickers (Bo-Bunny Press), brads and eyelets (ScrapArts), tags, Album: Joy Candrian

PAGE 41 BIRTHDAY GIRL

Album (Canson), paper (NRN Designs), stickers (NRN Designs), letter stickers (Making Memories, Wordsworth), Photos: Jill Neufeld

PAGE 45 CHRISTMAS

Album (Mrs. Grossman's), swirl stamp (PrintWorks), text stamp (Inkadinkado), month stamps (Making Memories), sticker letters (Wordsworth), 3-D stickers (Meri Meri), tags (DMD), brads (Limited Edition Rubberstamps), yarn

PAGE 45 A CHILD'S YEAR

Album (source unknown), papers and stickers (Provo Craft), Album: Kristen Jensen

PAGE 45 SEASON OF SPORTS

Album (Mrs. Grossman's), letter stickers (EK Success), 1" square punch, Photos: MaryJo Regier

PAGE 49 TEACHER

Album (Bound + D/termined), stickers (PSX Design), ink (Clearsnap), Photos: Shelley Balzer

PAGE 49 COACH

Album (DMD), Photos: Kris Perkins

PAGE 50 ALBUM COVER

Album (Awesome Albums), feather iron ons (Hirschberg Schutz & Co.), paper (Autumn Leaves), stamp (Acey Dacey), letter sticker (Colorbök), quote sticker (Wordsworth), "Treasure" sticker (Bo-Bunny Press)

PAGE 55 GIFT OF LOVE

Album (Pioneer), stamps (PrintWorks, Stampendous), ink (Clearsnap), embossing powder (Creative Beginnings), tags (Avery, DMD), photo corners (Canson), 3-D stickers (Meri Meri), vellum envelope (Robin's Nest), brad (Lasting Impressions), punch (Family Treasures), Photos: Nicole LaCour

PAGE 55 GARDENER'S ALBUM

Album and vellum paper (DMD), circle tags (Making Memories), ink (Hero Arts), scrapbook nails (Chatterbox), paper fiber (Emagination Crafts), Photo: Richard Gerbrandt

PAGE 59 INSPIRE

Album (DMD), stickers (Bo-Bunny Press, Stick 'Em Up, Wordsworth)

PAGE 59 WISDOM

Album (Rollabind), paper (7 Gypsies), ink (Clearsnap), embossing ink (Mark Enterprises), mini envelopes (DMD), photo corners (Canson), silk ribbon, Photos: Michele Gerbrandt

PAGE 59 FLOWERS & VERSE

Album (Kolo), papers (PrintWorks, PSX Design), paper fiber (Emagination Crafts), lettering template (Wordsworth), watercolor pencils, eyelet hole punch (Family Treasures), watercolor brush (EK Success)

PAGE 63 TRAVEL

Album (Canson), paper (DMD), corrugated paper (DMD), brads (Karen Foster Design), eyelets (Emagination Crafts), twine (7 Gypsies), Photos: Mike Haugen

PAGE 63 BLESSINGS

Album (handmade), paper (Bo-Bunny Press), mulberry paper (handmade), stickers (Bo Bunny Press, EK Success), photo corners (Pioneer), Album: Joy Candrian

PAGE 63 PIECES OF LIFE

Album (Books By Hand), mosaic tiles (EK Success), stickers (Making Memories), sticker envelope (EK Success), tags (Avery)

PAGE 67 FANTASY WORLD

Album (Close To My Heart), paper (Bazzill), photo paper (Printasia by Ilford), Zig writers (EK Success), chalk (Craf-T), Album: Becky Baack

PAGE 67 COMIC BOOK

Album (Kolo), patterned paper (Magenta), oval cartoon bubble punch (Emagination Crafts), watercolor pencils. Album: Pennie Stutzman

PAGE 67 NURSERY RHYMES

Album (Westrim), paper (O' Scrap/Imaginations), stamps (PSX Design), embroidery floss (DMC). Album: Shannon Taylor

PAGE 71 FRIEND

Album (Kolo), papers (Frances Meyer, Kangaroo and Joey, Provo Craft), Album: Julie Labuszewski

PAGE 71 FATHER'S DAY

Album (Close To My Heart), papers (Bazzill, Close To My Heart, Making Memories), stickers (Mrs. Grossman's), Zig pens (EK Success), ink (Clearsnap), brads (source unknown). Album: Becky Baack

PAGE 71 SAYING THANKS

Album (Kolo), lettering template (Wordsworth), chalk (Stampin' Up!)

PAGE 72 ALBUM COVER

Album (found book), papers (Books By Hand, DMD), vellum (DMD), definition stickers (Making Memories), flower stickers (K & Co.), metal frame (Making Memories), mesh (Magenta), ink (Clearsnap)

PAGE 77 KEY CHAIN

Album (handmade), letter stickers (Me & My Big Ideas, Mrs. Grossman's), laminate (Xyron), eyelets (Creative Imaginations), elastic (7 Gypsies), Photos: Elizabeth Friesen

PAGE 81 QUOTE CALENDAR

Album (Canson), paper (7 Gypsies), eyelets (Emagination Crafts), calendar (Payne Publishers), quote (Daisy D's), eyelet setter, hole punch, hammer, sandpaper

PAGE 81 COLLAGE CALENDAR

Album (DMD), paper (7 Gypsies), stamps (Close To My Heart, Stampendous), stickers (Autumn Leaves, Magenta), vellum paper (DMD), pages from old book

PAGE 84 TAGS

Tags (DMD), stickers (EK Success), stamps (PSX Design), ink (7 Gypsies), charms (Boutique Trims), beads (Darice)

Pam Klassen

Artistic ability runs in Pam's family—from parents to siblings to children. Art has always been a part of her life. Pam was also greatly inspired by a junior high school teacher who allowed experimentation with many mediums. In more recent times, she has been involved in the scrapbooking industry for eight years. Currently a freelance scrapbook designer and artist, her longtime interest in art led to a six-year position as Craft Editor at Memory Makers. Her page designs have been on numerous *Memory Makers* magazine and book covers as well as throughout the publications. Pam has created and directed the art in *Memory Makers Punch Your Art Out* books, *Creative Photo Cropping, Creative Paper Techniques* and *Borders, Corners & Titles*. Her page layouts have also been published in *Rubber Stamper Magazine*. She has been involved with exhibiting, demonstrating and teaching classes at numerous trade shows, including HIA and ACCI. Pam has also designed punches for Carl Manufacturing and created scrapbooks for the Susan G. Komen Breast Cancer Foundation. After creating dozens of small theme albums for friends, family members and as freelance work for others, she is excited and highly qualified to bring her tips, instruction and inspiration to the book you now hold. Pam lives and works on a fruit orchard in Reedley, California, with her husband, Tony, and daughters, Amanda and Jacquelyn. In her spare time, she enjoys remodeling projects, crafting, reading, woodworking, bicycling and going to the beach. Pam may be contacted by e-mail at klasspk@yahoo.com.

Contributing artists

Peggy Adair is a bank loan officer and branch manager who has been scrapbooking for six years. Married for 34 years with two married children and now grandchildren, she finds the time spent with family in Fort Smith, Arkansas to be among her greatest pleasures. adairpc@hotmail.com

Becky Baack is an artist, educator, wife and mother of two who resides in Aubrey, Texas. beckyb@joimail.com

For Debi, scrapbooking is the culmination of many years of involvement with memories and images. She started out as a professional children's photographer, followed by a career as a layout artist in the printing industry. And then she spent the next nine years as a one-person yearbook staff at her children's schools. Bringing these techniques, skill, love and flair to scrapbooking was natural for her, as she creates true works of heart. She resides in Scotts Valley, California. dboring1@aol.com

Joy Candrian is an artist, wife and mother of four adult children. She learned bookbinding as a youth in Portland, Oregon. Currently, she is a resident of Sandy, Utah. JoyCandrian@aol.com

Donna M. Dresp is an attorney, wife and mother of one who resides in Parma Heights, Ohio. donnadresp@cox.net

Kristen Jensen is a real estate developer, triathlete, wife and mother of two daughters residing in Woodinville, Washington.

Julie Labuszewski is raising three active boys with her husband, Tom, in Centennial, Colorado. She's a freelance writer, a recreational swimmer and enthusiastic scrapbooker. julielab@worldnet.att.net

Susan McFall lives in Reedley, California where she creates whimsical, hand-painted furniture, garden art and other fun stuff. honeybunart@comcast.net

Angela Siemens is a stay-at-home wife and mother, a passionate photographer, and is very addicted to scrapbooking with friends in Rosenort, Manitoba, Canada. pasiemens@conemail.com

Shannon Taylor calls herself a full-time keeper of memories. She is also a mother and part-time graphic designer who calls Bristol, Tennessee home. Scrappy3762@aol.com

Sources

The following companies manufacture products showcased on scrapbook pages within this book. Please check your local retailers to find these materials. We have made every attempt to properly credit the items mentioned in this book and apologize to those we may have missed.

3M Company
www.mmm.com

7 gypsies™
(800) 588-6707
www.7gypsies.com

Accu-Cut (wholesale only)
(800) 288-1670
www.accucut.com

All Night Media
(see Plaid Enterprises, Inc.)

American Crafts (wholesale only)
(800) 879-5185
www.americancrafts.com

American Tombow
(800) 835-3232
www.tombowusa.com

Anna Griffin, Inc. (wholesale only)
(888) 817-8170
www.annagriffin.com

Art Accents
(877) 733-8989
www.artaccents.net

Autumn Leaves (wholesale only)
(800) 588-6707
www.autumnleaves.com

Avery
(800) GO-AVERY
www.avery.com

Awesome Albums
(888) 300-3635
www.awesomealbums.com

Bazzill Basics Paper
(480) 558-8557
www.bazzillbasics.com

Bo Bunny Press
(801) 771-0481
www.bobunny.com

Books By Hand
(505) 255-3534
bbh@boyysbyhand.com

Bound + D/termined
(847) 696-1501
www.bound-determined.com

Boutique Trims, Inc.
(248) 437-2017
www.boutiquetrims.com

Boxer Scrapbook Productions
(888) 625-6255
www.boxerscrapbooks.com

Brother Industries, Ltd.
www.brother.com

Canson, Inc.®
(800) 628-9283
www.canson-us.com

Card Cafe Ltd., The
(260) 269-0662
www.thecardcafe.com

Carl Mfg. USA, Inc. (wholesale only)
(800) 257-4771
www.carl-products.com

Chatterbox, Inc.
(208) 939-9133
www.chatterboxinc.com

Clearsnap®, Inc. (wholesale only)
(800) 448-4862
www.clearsnap.com

Close to my Heart®
(888) 655-6552
www.closetomyheart.com

Club Scrap™, Inc.
(888) 634-9100
www.clubscrap.com

Colorbök™, Inc (wholesale only)
(800) 366-4660
www.colorbok.com

Colors By Design
(800) 832-8436
www.colorsbydesign.com

Craf-T Products
(507) 235-3996
www.craf-tproducts.com

Crafter's Workshop, The
(877) CRAFTER
www.thecraftersworkshop.com

Creative Beginings
(805) 772-9030
www.creativebeginnings.com

Creative Imaginations (wholesale only)
(800) 942-6487
www.cigift.com

Creative Impressions
(719) 596-4860
www.creativeimpressions.com

C-Thru® Ruler Company, The (wholesale only)
(800) 243-8419
www.cthruruler.com

Daisy D's Paper Company
(888) 601-8955
www.daisydspaper.com

Darice, Inc.
(800) 321-1494
www.darice.com

Delta Technical Coatings, Inc.
(800) 423-4135
www.deltacrafts.com

Design Originals
(800) 877-7820
www.d-originals.com

Destination Stickers and Stamps, Inc.
(866) 806-7826
www.destinationstickersandstamps.com

DMC Corp.
(973) 589-0606
www.dmc-usa.com

DMD Industries, Inc.
(800) 805-9890
www.dmdind.com

Dragon Ink- no contact info. available

EK Success™ ,Ltd. (wholesale only)
(800) 524-1349
www.eksuccess.com

Ellison® Craft and Design
(800) 253-2238
www.ellison.com

Emagination Crafts, Inc.
(630) 833-9521
www.emaginationcrafts.com

Family Archives, The
(604) 826-3339
www.heritagescrapbooks.com

Family Treasures, Inc.®
(no longer in business)

Fiber Scraps
(215) 230-4905
www.fiberscraps.com

Frances Meyer, Inc.
(800) 372-6237
www.francesmeyer.com

Glitterex Corp.- no contact info. available

Global Solutions
(206) 343-5210
www.globalsolutionsonline.com

Graphic Products Corp.
(800) 323-1660
www.gdcpapers.com

Halcraft USA, Inc.
(212) 367-1580
www.halcraft.com

Handmade Scraps, Inc.
www.handmadescraps.com

Hero Arts® Rubber Stamps, Inc.
(800) 822-4376
www.heroarts.com

Hirschberg Schutz & Co. (wholesale only)
(800) 221-8640

Hot Off The Press, Inc.
(800) 227-9595
www.paperpizazz.com

Ilford Imaging USA, Inc.
(888) 727-4751
www.printasiafun.com

Inkadinkado® Rubber Stamps
(800) 888-4652
www.inkadinkado.com

Inkerbelle- no contact info. available

International Paper
www.ippaper.com

JewelCraft, LLC
(201) 223-0804
www.jewelcraft.biz

JudiKins
(310) 515 1115
www.judikins.com

K & Company
(888) 244-2083
www.kandcompany.com

Kangaroo & Joey (wholesale only)
(480) 460-4841
www.kangarooandjoey.com

Karen Foster Design™ (wholesale only)
(801) 451-9779
www.karenfosterdesign.com

Kolo™, LLC
(888) 828-0367
www.kolo-usa.com

Lasting Impressions for Paper, Inc.
(801) 298-1979
www.lastingimpressions.com

Limited Edition Rubberstamps
(650) 594-4242
www.limitededitionrs.com

Magenta Rubber Stamps
(wholesale only)
(800) 565-5254
www.magentarubberstamps.com

Magic Scraps™
(972) 238-1838
www.magicscraps.com

Making Memories
(800) 286-5263
www.makingmemories.com

Mark Enterprises (see Stampendous!)

Marvy® Uchida (wholesale only)
(800) 541-5877
www.uchida.com

me and my BIG ideas (wholesale only)
(949) 589-4607
www.meandmybigideas.com

Meri Meri (wholesale only)
(650) 525-9200
www.merimeri.com

Mrs. Grossman's Paper Co.
(wholesale only)
(800) 429-4549
www.mrsgrossmans.com

Mustard Moon
(408) 229-8542
www.mustardmoon.com

NRN Designs
(800) 421-6988
www.nrndesigns.com

O'Scrap!/Imaginations!
(801) 225-6015
www.imaginations-inc.com

Paper Adventures (wholesale only)
(800) 727-0699
www.paperadventures.com

Paper Garden, The (wholesale only)
(702) 639-1956
www.mypapergarden.com

Papers by Catherine
(713) 723-3334
www.papersbycatherine.com

Payne Publishers, Inc.
www.paynepub.com

Pioneer Photo Albums, Inc.
(800) 366-3686
www.pioneerphotoalbums.com

Plaid Enterprises, Inc.
(800) 842-2883
www.plaidonline.com

Polaroid Corporation
www.polaroid.com

Printasia (see Ilford Imaging)

PrintWorks
(800) 854-6558
www.printworkscollections.com

Provo Craft® (wholesale only)
(888) 577-3545
www.provocraft.com

PSX Design™
(800) 782-6748
www.psxdesign.com

Reminiscence Papers
(503) 246-9681
www.reminiscencepapers.com

Robin's Nest Press, The (wholesale only)
(435) 789-5387
www.robinsnest-scrapbook.com

Rollabind®, Inc.
(800) 438-3542
www.rollabind.com

Running Rhino and Co.
(800) 574-4665
www.runningrhino.com

Sakura of America
(800) 776-6257
www.gellyroll.com

Sandylion Sticker Designs
(wholesale only)
(800) 387-4215
www.sandylion.com

Scrap-Ease® (What's New LTD)
(wholesale only)
(800) 272-3874
www.whatsnewltd.com

ScrapArts
(503) 631-4893
www.scraparts.com

Scrappin' Dreams
(417) 831-1882
www.scrappindreams.com

Sizzix
(866) 742-4447
www.sizzix.com

Staedtler® Inc.
(800) 927-7723
www.staedtler-usa.com

Stampa Rosa (no longer in business)

Stampendous!®
(800) 869-0474
www.stampendous.com

Stampin' Up!®
(800) 782-6787
www.stampinup.com

Stick' em Up- no contact info. available

Strathmore (see International Paper)

Sulyn Industries, Inc.
(954) 755-2311
www.sulyn.com

Sweetwater
(970) 867-4428
www.sweetwaterscrapbook.com

Therm O Web, Inc. (wholesale only)
(800) 323-0799
www.thermoweb.com

Uptown Design Company™
(253) 925-1000
www.uptowndesign.com

Westrim® Crafts
(800) 727-2727
www.westrimcrafts.com

Wish in the Wind
(757) 564-6400
www.wishinthewind.com

Wordsworth Stamps
(719) 282-3495
www.wordsworthstamps.com

Xyron, Inc.
(800) 793-3523
www.xyron.com

Index